THE CHESAPEAKE
COOKBOOK

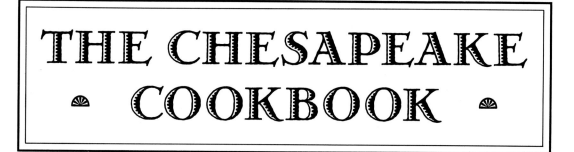

PHOTOGRAPHS BY
MICHAEL SKOTT

DESIGNED BY
GINA DAVIS

THE CHESAPEAKE · COOKBOOK ·

SUSAN BELSINGER AND
CAROLYN DILLE

Clarkson N. Potter, Inc./Publishers

Above all to Audrey and Robert,

who know and who care;

to past Chesapeake cooks, in fond memory;

and to future Chesapeake cooks,

especially Lucie, with fond hopes

Published by Clarkson N. Potter, Inc., 201 East 50th Street,
New York, New York 10022

CLARKSON N. POTTER, POTTER and colophon are
trademarks of Clarkson N. Potter, Inc.
Manufactured in Japan
Library of Congress Cataloging-in-Publication Data
Belsinger, Susan.
The Chesapeake cookbook/by Susan Belsinger and
Carolyn Dille.
p. cm.
Includes index.
1. Cookery—Chesapeake Bay (Md. and Va.)
2. Cookery, Marine.
I. Dille, Carolyn. II. Title.
TX715.B465 1989
641.59752'—dc19   88–26903
ISBN 0-517-58164-7   CIP
10 9 8 7 6 5 4 3 2 1
First Edition

ACKNOWLEDGMENTS

Many people showed us characteristic Chesapeake hospitality and were generous with their help; their participation made writing this book a pleasure.

Linda Hayes, our agent, has our warm and grateful thanks for her enthusiasm and involvement much beyond an agent's imperative.

We will be forever grateful for the good humor and unfailing support of our families: Robert and Audrey Belsinger, Sally Belsinger, Doneth and David Hinkleman, Louanne Sargent, Thomas Sargent, Warren and Marguerite Sargent, and Dick Walvis.

Our special thanks to friends and acquaintances who contributed to this book in so many ways: Donald Albright, George Barnard, Dr. and Mrs. Edward Besson, Lena Caron, Ed, Maggie, and Eddie Cutts, Golda and Jim Davis, Ron Day, Joyce and Tom DeBaggio, Katherine Eichnor, Gil Feldman, Marty Feldman, Mrs. Ginny Glenn, Harvey Goolsby, Annette Hale, Deborah Hall, Ellen Hartge, John, Elizabeth, and Bill Hartge, Tracy Jones, Gary Keyes, Dan and Barbara Kral, Johnny Bill Lenton, David Lenz, Tom Lindsay, Sean Mann, Carol Martielli, Claire and John Martielli, MaryAnn McDonald, Betty Ann and Ed McGinty, Laurence Moore, Davina and Louis Placella, Tatiana and Joe Seelinger, Tommy Stanfield, Karen Stanford, John Valiant, Michael Wettach, and Ivy Williams.

We would also like to thank Dr. and Mrs. John Martielli, Craig O'Donnell and Deborah Hall, Chuck Sharp and Denise Doerer, and the owners of By His Grace, Ellerslie, and Riverside for graciously opening their homes to our photographer; the Cutts and Case Boatyard of Oxford, Maryland, for permitting the use of the yachts *Spell Bound* and *Jeanne,* and Eddie Cutts for giving us such a good sail; the managers of Chesapeake Bay Maritime Museum, St. Michaels, Maryland; Howard County Hunt Club, Ellicott City, Maryland; Ladew Topiary Gardens, Monkton, Maryland; Larriland Farm, Woodbine, Maryland; Little Round Bay Neighborhood Dock, Severna Park, Maryland; St. Mary's County Oyster Festival, Leonardtown, Maryland; Sharp Farm, Glenwood, Maryland, and Waterford Farm, Brookeville, Maryland, who cordially made the arrangements for photographing these sites: Larkspur: Floral design by Carol B. Westerlund, Whitehall, Maryland; Good Earth Produce, Olney, Maryland; Wilhide's Flowers, Ellicott City, Maryland; and Deborah Hall for help in providing or arranging flowers; Michael Weal, manager of the Forest Motel, and Tom Burke, administrator of the St. Mary's County Oyster Festival, for arranging accommodations for our photographic team at the Forest Motel, Ellicott City, Maryland, and the Patuxent Inn, Lexington Park, Maryland; Country Cottage, Ellicott City, Maryland; Gaines McHale Antiques, Cockeysville, Maryland; Tatiana, Glenwood, Maryland; The Iron Rail, Ellicott City, Maryland, and, in New York City, the Frank McIntosh Shop at Henri Bendel, American Antiques and Quilts, Wolfman Gold & Good, and Mottahedeh and Co., for cordially lending us props for our photography sessions.

Gigi Dux of the Delaware State Travel Service has our heartfelt thanks for giving us so much help and information concerning Delaware people, places, and food. For providing us with the finest Chesapeake foodstuffs we thank the generous people at Larriland Farm, Woodbine, Maryland; Sharp Farm, Glenwood, Maryland; and The Crab Claw Restaurant, St. Michaels, Maryland. Finally, we are especially thankful to Noreen Eberly of the Maryland Office of Seafood and Marketing, Annapolis, Maryland, for her advice and her efforts to provide us with the best of the Bay's seafood.

CONTENTS

CHESAPEAKE RECIPES

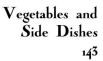

INTRODUCTION

The rows of gleaming oysters on ice, the glisten of fresh fish, the fire engine glow of steamed crabs, the piles of podded lima beans, the matte green of corn husks and the pearly pale kernels of Silver Queen corn, the smell of freshly grated coconut, the aromatic pungency of horseradish root, the sweetly scented flesh of Eastern Shore cantaloupe, the strawberries and raspberries to inspire perfumers, the heady fragrance of peaches—these are the impressions one receives in the Lexington Market of Baltimore, Maryland. The oldest continuously operated city market in the United States palpably introduces the real-life cornucopia that furnishes the Chesapeake region.

Outside the cities, country and surburban dwellers around the Chesapeake Bay buy the same fresh foodstuffs at vegetable stands, seafood and crab shacks, and from small refrigerated trucks that follow regular neighborhood routes. The large inventory that supplies all these retailers comes from the Eastern Shore of Maryland and from Delaware across the Bay, from the inlets, islands, banks, and shores of Virginia and Maryland, where the watermen and fishermen ply, from the central and southern

Maryland truck farms. The land and water have provided residents from precolonial times to the present with an abundance of provender, both cultivated and wild. In the late twentieth century you could certainly find foodstuffs from New Jersey, South Carolina, or California in the Chesapeake Bay area, but the region is remarkably self-sufficient and its inhabitants still prize localism.

The homogenization so prevalent in most local cooking across the United States, especially during the twentieth century, has been resisted here to a great extent. Maryland's Smith Islanders still make crab cakes their way, which are as different from those in Easton, on the Eastern Shore, as those are from Baltimore's. Tidewater Virginia puts Smithfield ham in its version of Crab Imperial, while those of Maryland often include green pepper. Oyster stew is made with milk or cream on the mainland. On the dredge (pronounced *drudge*) boats—the oyster-gathering boats—it is made with evaporated milk, potatoes, and salt pork, ingredients that keep well when the boats are out for a week or so, and that provide the hearty nourishment necessary to sustain heavy work schedules.

The land that bounds the Chesapeake was codified after the American Revolution into the states of Maryland, Virginia, and Delaware. The peninsula between the Chesapeake and Delaware bays is divided among the three states, with Delaware and Maryland splitting the main portion about equally and the southern tip belonging to Virginia. Although Delaware does not touch Chesapeake Bay, its own bay has the same varieties of oysters and crabs found in the Chesapeake. Many specialties of Maryland's Eastern Shore and Delaware are a matter of local variations. Virginia does not lay claim to as much of the Chesapeake shoreline; but, although peninsular and Tidewater Virginia are a small part of the state's area, they have produced fascinating combinations of foods, such as peanut and oyster stuffing for turkey.

Diverse immigrants—the English, Germans, Jews, Poles, Italians, and black Africans (who came originally as slaves)—settled in the Chesapeake from colonial times to the end of the nineteenth century and their contributions have also enriched the Chesapeake's cuisine. Their judicious use of spices and herbs is an example of how this melding has produced dishes difficult to improve. The complex spice blends that are used to season seafood and a range of other foods are immediately recognizable for their Chesapeake flavor, distinct from Cajun, Creole, or Chinese. Probably the taste for pepper with seafood came from the black cooks. The use of celery seed in these blends points in a different direction, to the German cooks, while mustard and bay leaves indicate the influence of the English, who planted kitchen herbs such as mar-joram, thyme, sage, tarra-gon, and savory. Even today Maryland, Delaware, and Virginia are home to a number of thriving herb farms, and spices are still an important commodity for the region.

Just as in the early twentieth century Eastern Europeans and Southern Italians brought what were considered exotic foods and flavorings—Polish sausage, pizza, and olives—so the more recent immigrants from the Far East and Central America are contributing their distinctive flavorings and dishes, such as coriander leaf or black beans with soft shell crabs.

Still, the most typical foods—coleslaw, corn bread, stewed tomatoes, oysters and clams on the half shell, steamed crabs, roast goose, and baked fish—remain simple and tasty, with little of the overelaboration of class-conscious or restaurant-dominated cuisines. Most of the immigrants, whatever their point of origin, have been middle and working class, with a peasant's view of food: respect even in the face of abundance; frugality of technique and ingredients; appreciation of natural flavor.

The heartland of this region of rolling hills, flatlands, rivers, and marshes is the Chesapeake Bay, crossed and recrossed by the Algonquin Indians long before the European immigrants came to it. The Maryland portion of the Chesapeake peninsula is called the Eastern Shore, with the lion's share of inlets, estuaries, shoreline, and marshland. Most of the watermen come from this side or from the islands in the Bay. Dr. Ed Besson is an Eastern Shore native who has shared much of the Shore's rich food lore with us. When, in his soft, slightly accented voice, he recalls the rituals and rhythms of preparing, hunting, and enjoying the local food, it is with the grace of a natural storyteller.

Summer—the high sea-son—brought soft and hard crabs, clams, eels, frogs' legs, fatbacks (a kind of mul-let), succotash, red tomatoes sprinkled with brown sugar, head lettuce salad, and pat-typan squash. Saturday sum-mer supper was fried fish, corn bread, tomato salad, and homemade vanilla ice cream.

Fall was the time when the much-anticipated oyster harvest began. Dr. Besson's favorite preparation is still roasted oysters, which he insists must be done over an open fire for the flavor that will make gluttons of even moderate eaters. A popular church supper dish was a combination of chicken salad and fried oysters. The oysters were dipped in beaten egg, then in fine cracker crumbs, and fried in lard or vegetable oil. For Thanksgiving dinner, oysters were scalloped: simply layers of oysters sprinkled lightly with crushed saltine crackers, with cream from the cow and oyster liquor poured over.

Rabbit and squirrel, usually floured, fried, and fricasseed at the end of the cooking with cream gravy, also made fall and winter dinners. Thanksgiving dinner always included mashed parsnips and cooked greens, as salad greens were for summer eating. Black walnuts were gathered to make cakes and cookies. Serious baking began after the summer's heat—cinnamon buns, apple pie, mince pie, molasses cake.

Winter was hog-butchering season, time for cold-smoking the hams and making sausage, which was flavored with black pepper and dried sage. Gunning, as hunting is called on the Shore, brought Canada geese and black and mallard ducks, usually hung for a week, then roasted plain. The Friday night winter meal was baked navy beans prepared with onions, tomatoes, and molasses, and sweat pone, a mixture of cooked cornmeal mush and beaten eggs steamed in a buttered dish.

The finest early spring or late winter dish was the famed Maryland terrapin stew, but muskrat-trapping provided a seasonal treat that tastes like canvasback duck. Three or four were put in a pot with a hambone to season, a little water and salt and pepper, then covered with turnip greens and steam-braised until tender.

Today, two concerns influence Chesapeake cooking. The first is an increasing awareness of the relationship of diet to health. Cooks are lightening dishes, principally by using less fat. In earlier times, when the majority of families kept hogs and did much more strenuous labor than we now do, it made sense to use lard as the main cooking fat. Likewise, butter and cream were valuable for enriching flavor and adding necessary calories. Pure lard is hard to find today, and though dairy products are still of fine quality, they are used in lesser quantities. The second is concern over the erratic but declining amounts of seafood available in the Chesapeake for landing —the commercial catch—in recent years. The region's citizens, as well as local, state, and federal officials and those who earn their living from the water, have turned their concentration to keeping the Chesapeake full of marine life. Substantial cooperation among the states whose shores or rivers form the Bay has become important and is being implemented in many ways, from sea bass hatchery programs to increasingly stringent antipollution laws. For information on projects to protect the Chesapeake, contact Maryland Governor W. Donald Schaefer's office at (301) 974-5300, State House, Annapolis, MD 21401.

To present the best of an area with such a diversity of food traditions, we have worked with many sources: talented cooks, friends and acquaintances, and historical cookbooks. Audrey and Robert Belsinger, Susan's mother and father, who are third-generation Baltimoreans, have provided us with the deepest insights. Their knowledge of Chesapeake foodstuffs—from truck farm produce to the game and fish Robert takes every season—is broad, and their love of cooking is great. They, along with the Bessons, and other families and friends, contributed heirloom recipes to this book. Some dishes—such as Crab Soup, Scalloped Oysters, and Stuffed Ham—have such long histories that they represent collective judgments of the best preparations. Still, individual cooks add touches that distinguish the dishes and allow them to rise above the ordinary.

We are proud to offer a selection of the best new and time-honored recipes of the region. The cooks who developed such an individual and distinctive cuisine are well served by the present generation of cooks, who bring contemporary ideas but keep the high standards of the past. For the future, we think the dedication to hard work, openness to the exchange of techniques and ideas, and love of place will promote, as earlier, new dishes that respect the long traditions of the finest Chesapeake cookery. We hope you find ample inspiration to include this varied and genuine regional cuisine in your culinary repertoire.

FOODS FROM THE LAND AND THE BAY

T

he Chesapeake region depends much on its local food production. Agricultural livelihoods—fishing, oystering, crabbing, and farming—have been followed for generations. Though their absolute numbers have declined, oystermen, crabmen, fishermen, and farmers contribute significantly to the economy of the Chesapeake area, as well as to its distinctive cooking traditions. The harvests of shellfish and fish are not only appreciated by the people here, but find worldwide markets.

In this section we discuss the particularly important foods produced here, as well as some ingredients and prepared foods that give dishes a characteristic Chesapeake flavor. Though we do not have space to cover everything from this generally self-sufficient region, you will find that there is much more to Chesapeake food than crab and corn. In addition to description, the glossary provides helpful information on storing, cleaning, and preparing the principal foodstuffs of the region.

Because of the close link between production and consumption, seasonal specialties still govern the patterns of food selection and menu-planning. Residents eagerly await spring, which brings soft-shell crabs, a variety of berries, and asparagus. Summer is the great season of abundance, with hard shell steamer crabs, finfish of all kinds, corn, tomatoes, lettuce and herbs, melons, and peaches. In autumn, new crop apples are at the top of everyone's list; for the foragers and hunters there are wild persimmons, wild mushrooms, and game. Winter's most prized fresh food is the Chesapeake oyster. For hearty cold-weather meals, people use fruits and vegetables preserved in summer and hams cured in fall. The variety of foods available throughout the year ensures that Chesapeake menus—such as the seven menus beginning on page 27—are well balanced, with pride of place given to whichever food is at its peak.

COUNTY FAIR

County fairs are both fun and serious business for county residents. There are numerous entry categories, from garden flowers and vegetables to farm crops and livestock, baked goods and preserves to arts and crafts. 4H'ers play a large part in the region's county fairs. They enter livestock large and small—from pigs and cows to rabbits and ducks. All animals are judged on fineness of breed, size, and vitality.

Youngsters put their prized pigs, above far left, through the paces in the Howard County Fair 4H competition.

Balloons and grown-ups present obstacles for little ones, above left.

Flower entries range from single blossoms of a wide variety of annuals and perennials to displays of miniatures, mixed bouquets, and monochromatic arrangements, above.

This melon and pumpkin, far left, were named champion for their size, shape, color, and ripeness.

High school girls dressed as clowns, left, entertain the youngsters.

11

FROM THE LAND

APPLES

The most popular eating, cooking, and cider apple in the region is the Stayman Winesap, marketed also as the Stayman or the Winesap. Its firm, perfumed flesh is excellent for pies, cakes, and applesauce. We substitute the crisp McIntosh if we can't find the Stayman.

CHESAPEAKE SEAFOOD SEASONING

Chesapeake-style seafood seasoning for steamed crabs is attributed to the black cooks of the nineteenth century; it struck a responsive chord in all steamed-crab eaters. Until the 1930s, home cooks made their own blends, while crab houses and restaurants commissioned theirs from the region's many spice merchants. Made from a variety of spices and herbs, with paprika, cayenne, black pepper, bay leaves, and celery seed predominant, the seasoning was also used for other varieties of seafood, though it was, and still is, most prevalent in blue crab dishes.

In 1939, the Baltimore Spice Company perfected a blend of 13 spices, marketed as Old Bay® seasoning. It is still the most popular, both in the region and nationwide, though it does have its competitors, notably the McCormick and Wye River brands. Chesapeake restaurants and crab houses continue to have their own blends specially made, and natives passionately defend their favorite brands. We find that any blend adds flavor, but we do confess that Old Bay is our favorite, and it is the one used for the recipes in this book.

CORN

The preferred eating corn here is, by far, the white variety called Silver Queen. It is exceptionally sweet and tender with fine corn flavor. Choose corn with filled-out ears, preferably from a supplier who can tell you when it was picked. If the corn was harvested at the proper stage, the tassels should be light brown and still supple.

CORNMEAL

We recommend stone-ground cornmeal for its flavor, though degerminated (germ removed) cornmeal has a longer storage life. Store stone-ground cornmeal in the refrigerator if you do not use it often. White and yellow cornmeal are equally popular for both traditional and modern recipes.

GAME MEAT

Deer, rabbit, squirrel, and muskrat are hunted in season and provide tasty eating for many Chesapeake families. A 100-pound deer will yield about 60 pounds of venison. Yearlings provide the most tender meat; an older deer will be tougher. The filet or loin are the best cuts, often marinated in red wine and then roasted or grilled. Steaks are usually pan-braised or grilled, and lesser cuts are ground or used for stews. Muskrat, rabbit, and squirrel are pan-braised or stewed, usually with wine and herbs.

GAME BIRDS

Most game birds in the Chesapeake region are waterfowl, though quail, dove, and pheasant are also prized for the table. All game birds are prepared rather simply, either roasted, grilled, or pan-fried, and served with light sauces. Recipes for domestic duck and goose are relatively few, probably because game birds are so plentiful and hunting is such a strong tradition.

CANADA GOOSE has always been the most desirable game bird in the Chesapeake region. The beautiful Canada geese spend much of their winter lives in the cornfields or in the waters of the Eastern Shore of Maryland. Goose-hunting is sport for some, and a way of life for many shore men. During the season, the limit per person is three geese a day. They range in weight from 10 to 13 pounds unplucked, or 4 to 6 pounds table-dressed. Hunters commonly hire local pluckers, who pluck and clean the day's bag for a small fee. When roasted, the Canada goose has dark meat with a rich, not overly gamy, flavor.

DUCK, including the canvasback, mallard, and black duck, hold an important place in Chesapeake cuisine. They are similar in size and weight, 3 to 4 pounds table-dressed, and in the pronounced flavor of their dark meat; some hunters consider the black duck the best eating because it seldom has any trace of muddy flavor. Duck is roasted or pan-braised, and it is usually served with a sauce made either with red wine and herbs, or port wine and currant jelly.

HAM

Just a generation ago, most country families around the Chesapeake raised and butchered their own hogs. Even today, when ham is usually prepared commercially, it is a much-favored staple for many people. There are numerous methods for curing a country ham, from soaking in brine and cold-smoking to salt- or sugar-curing. Once the ham is cured it may be served in many ways: sliced thin and brought to the table cold as a main course or in sandwiches; cut into steaks, fried, and accompanied by pan gravy; or turned into meat loaf or deviled ham, to name a few. A southern Maryland specialty is Stuffed Ham. The ham traditionally used for this dish is corned, that is, brined with spices and herbs. Since it is quite perishable, it is rarely found outside the area. If you substitute another kind of ham, be sure it does not have a strong flavor of either smoke-cure or honey.

HORSERADISH

The long brown taproots used for making horseradish come from a perennial (*Amoracia rusticana*) that is related to the mustard family. The Chesapeake climate is ideal for growing this pungent root. Horseradish is most pungent when used fresh, as it progressively loses its bite during storage. It should be grated just before needed, unless it is to be mixed in a sauce or prepared with vinegar. We prefer to use only fresh horseradish in many of our recipes, but prepared horseradish may be substituted. A ratio of 4 parts prepared horseradish to 3 parts freshly grated horseradish will approximate the pungency of all fresh. Since prepared horseradish is preserved with vinegar, adjust the amounts of lemon juice or vinegar to taste if any is called for in the recipe.

LIMA BEANS

Fordhook lima beans are raised and sold fresh in the Chesapeake Bay area chiefly to prepare succotash, a popular regional specialty derived from a Native American dish. In its simplest form, succotash is just-picked corn, tender fresh lima beans, and salt. Cream, butter, or pepper are sometimes added, but no other vegetables.

MELONS

The inland Chesapeake region, especially the Eastern Shore and Delaware, is prime melon-growing territory, with cantaloupe, honeydew, and watermelon the major crops. Of the hundreds of varieties of melons, natives agree that nothing compares with the intensely perfumed Eastern Shore cantaloupe. Two of the most popular watermelons are Crimson Sweets and Sugar Babies.

MOLASSES

The use of molasses in Chesapeake cooking dates from the seventeenth century, when Baltimore was a principal port for Caribbean and West

Ripe Silver Queen corn and cantaloupes are ready for market.

Home-grown flowers can be arranged by even the
youngest gardener.

Indian trade. For about 150 years molasses was used as the main sweetener, and it is still popular, especially in cornmeal dishes. Any type of molasses, dark or light, sulfured or unsulfured, may be used in our recipes. Keep in mind that dark molasses is much stronger in flavor than light; use a bit less or expect a heavier taste.

OILS AND FATS

Many of the traditional recipes appearing in this book originally called for vegetable oil or lard. We give a choice of oils in those recipes where substitutions can be made. Some recipes may specify peanut oil because of its high smoking point. If olive oil is listed with no alternative, we are depending on it for flavor. As it is hard to find good-quality lard today, we use oil or butter in breads and for frying, and vegetable shortening in pie crusts (the hydrogenated oils produce a flakier crust).

PERSIMMONS

Wild persimmons (*Diospyros virginiana*) are the fruits of trees native to this region. The Algonquin Indians instructed the settlers on the uses and harvest of persimmons; the fruit immediately found a place in the settlers' diets and was commonly used in breads and puddings. The wild fruit *must* be harvested after a killing frost, which alters its chemical structure: underripe persimmons contain an astringent compound that causes the mouth to pucker. Most of the persimmons found in markets today are the *Diospyros kaki* variety. Both wild and cultivated varieties must be perfectly ripe for the characteristic luscious, rich, sweet flavor. To choose the best fruit, look for a bright orange-red color, with no yellow, and no bad spots. The persimmon may be streaked with black. The fruit will be soft—in fact, a dead-ripe persimmon should be very soft to the touch, almost squishy, and even a little shriveled. If the fruit is not quite ripe, let it sit at room temperature for a few days until soft.

SAUERKRAUT

The sauerkraut crock that was a part of most Chesapeake kitchens disappeared as fresh home-style sauerkraut became available in city markets around the region. This kind of sauerkraut continues to be popular as a winter vegetable because its flavor and texture are fresher and crisper than that of commercially canned sauerkraut. If you cannot find fresh bulk sauerkraut in your area, look for sauerkraut in plastic packages or in glass jars. Taste the packed sauerkraut; rinse and drain it if it tastes sharp or tinny.

TOMATOES

A summer-ripe tomato is incomparable, but an Eastern Shore summer-ripe tomato is truly in a class by itself. Hot, humid summers and good soil allow Delmarva Peninsula and mainland Maryland farmers to provide area residents with succulent tomatoes from about July 1 through the summer. Sandwiches consisting only of thick-sliced tomatoes seasoned with salt and pepper between two slices of bread, and perhaps a bit of mayonnaise, are the daily lunches for many natives during this period. Mountain Pride and PikRed, which have an excellent balance of sweetness and acidity, are the main commercial varieties. Store ripe tomatoes at cool room temperature; refrigeration dulls their flavor dramatically.

WINES

Viticulture and wine-making have been seriously pursued in this region since Thomas Jefferson's day. Jefferson imported French grape cultivars and experimented with native grapes for wine production. Today, both Maryland and Virginia produce some fine table wines, notably Chardonnay, American and Johannisberg Riesling, Seyval Blanc, and Cabernet Sauvignon. They are worth asking for in your wine shop, as they add another dimension to Chesapeake food, whether used in recipes or as an accompaniment to meals. If you cannot find them, substitute other American or imported wines of the types mentioned.

FROM THE BAY

CLAMS

The Chesapeake offers a variety of both soft and hard shell clams. The soft shell clam, also referred to as the manninose, maninose, manos, or long-neck, has a thin, elongated shell and is good deep-fried or steamed. Hard shell clams, eaten both cooked and raw, are sold in several sizes. Littlenecks, the smallest, and cherrystones, the next size larger, are delicious on the half shell, while the very large chowder clams are used for soups and sauces. Other clams, notably the surf, and the quahog or Mahagony, are important to the canned clam industry, but are seldom found in retail markets because they are difficult to open and their flavor is not as fine as that of other clams.

Clams may be purchased either live (in the shell), shucked, canned, or frozen. Be sure that the shells of live clams are tightly closed; discard any that are not. Shucked clams should be plump and their liquid clear. Canned and frozen clams, while not as flavorful as the fresh, may be used in recipes to be cooked. All live clams, especially soft shells, may be sandy. We let them disgorge their sand by putting them in a fresh cold water bath with a little cornmeal. This does work, but the clams should be checked after they are opened, and rinsed if necessary. It is a good idea to check for sand even in canned or frozen clams.

To shuck hard shell clams, you'll need a clam knife, a heavy glove or oven mitt, and a towel for protection. With the clam knife, find an opening where the two shells meet opposite the hinge. Hold the clam in your gloved hand on the towel and work the knife into the opening. Once the knife is inserted, turn it so that it is parallel to the hinge and move it firmly toward the hinge. Bend the top shell back and run the knife under the clam to loosen it from the top and bottom shells. With the tip of the knife remove any bits of shell or sand. Remove the top shells for half-shell presentation. Nestle the clams on a bed of crushed ice or rock salt to help contain their juices. Serve all clams, raw or cooked, as soon as possible.

To shuck and clean soft shell clams, insert a clam knife in the shell opening at the neck. Keeping the knife parallel to the top shell, carefully run it along the shell and free the clam. The shells are very brittle, so check the meat for broken bits of shell. If you intend to fry the clams, the tough necks should be discarded.

If soft shell clams are to be steamed, scrub the shells thoroughly and leave the clams unshucked. Many people remove the black skin from the necks of steamed clams and eat the necks along with the clams.

CRABS

Blue crabs (*Callinectus sapidus*) have brought fame to the Chesapeake Bay, and rightly so—we think that they are the best-tasting crab available. The sweet, firm meat is used in specialty dishes of the region, from Crab Imperials and salads to crab cakes and soups. Steamed hard crab with Chesapeake seafood seasoning is the most popular form of crab-eating here. The spicy seasoning blend is an excellent contrast to the sweet, succulent crabmeat.

HARD SHELL CRABS are steamed, then "picked" with a small, sharp knife with a heavy handle. To pick a steamed crab Chesapeake-style, turn the crab on its back and remove the U- or V-shaped apron with your hands, pulling up the point of the V. Break off the legs. Remove the top shell from the body with your hands. Cut the face area from the body with a knife. Remove the gills from both sides of the body, and cut or break the body in half. Many people use little wooden mallets to crack the remaining shell, but we find this results in rather bruised crabmeat with bits of shell in it. Loosen and cut away the thin pearly white cartilage to expose the meat.

OYSTER FESTIVAL

An annual two-day oyster festival is held in St. Mary's County each October that attracts entrants for the National Oyster Shucking Championship from all the oyster-farming states.

Oysters harvested from Potomac and Chesapeake waters for the shucking contest. Bushels of fresh oysters, left, are also prepared for the public—on the half shell, fried, and in oyster sandwiches.

Oyster lovers at St. Mary's County fairgrounds, below, are ready to root for their favorite contestants.

Shuckers wait for the starting gun, right, to begin the contest; at stake is the grand prize, a trip to Ireland to compete in the International Shucking Contest.

Shucking speed and clean, plump oysters, below right, are what the judges look for in determining the winning entrants.

The prizewinners proudly display their work, below far right.

This procedure will take some practice before you become proficient, but after opening several crabs you will learn how the segments of the crab join together, and will be able to pinpoint the large chunks of body meat. Clean the chambers of meat, and eat the soft yellowish crab "butter" or "mustard." To pick the legs and claws, turn them so that the softer, lighter-colored undersides are facing you and tap with the knife handle or with a mallet. Remove the meat with a knife point or your fingers.

Crab houses cover their tables with brown paper and newspaper and provide crab pickers with plenty of paper napkins or paper towels. Finger-licking is *de rigueur*, and is the best way to taste the crab seasoning along with the crab.

Whole cooked blue crabs are sold in many markets in the region. If you buy both cooked and live crabs, be sure to store them separately. If they are stored so that they come in contact, cross-contamination between the naturally occurring bacteria on raw and cooked foods may take place, and could result in illness after the crabs are eaten.

Cooked blue crab is also available already picked. During the summer the meat is usually sold fresh and is very perishable. It is also sold pasteurized, a process developed and perfected by Byrd, Inc., a seafood company in Crisfield, Maryland. This form of crabmeat has no additives and must be kept refrigerated. We have found it quite tasty and use it in cooked dishes. We do not freeze any crabmeat, fresh or pasteurized, since it ruins the texture.

Picked crab is graded and priced according to the size of the lumps of meat. Lump or backfin (the name depending on the packer) is the choicest grade, made up of large whole chunks of body meat. Special grade combines chunks and small bits or flakes of body meat. Other grades are regular, consisting of flakes or small bits of body meat, and claw, meat from the claws only. Before you use picked crab, remove any pieces of cartilage.

SOFT SHELL CRABS, often called peelers or green crabs, are blue crabs in the molting stage. Ten to fourteen days before a crab is about to shed its shell, it will begin to feed furiously, then head for shallow waters where it can safely hide in the seaweed. This is the best time for a crabber to catch the crabs, place them in a pen, and hold them until they molt. The crab is called a buster during this arduous process of breaking loose from its shell, which takes about three hours. For two days or so after molting, the crab is a soft shell crab, perfect for eating.

Soft shell crabs should be alive when you buy them. They must be dressed before cooking, a service fishmongers provide. Most Chesapeake natives dress their own crabs because the closer to cooking time the crab is dressed, the more succulent and flavorful it is. To dress a soft crab, cut off the face, just behind the eyes, with a sharp knife or scissors. Turn the crab belly side up and remove the apron. Next, lift the pointed flaps on each side of the crab and remove the spongy gills with the knife. Rinse the gill area if it is sandy. The soft crab is now dressed and should be placed on a dish so that the head region is angled upward to keep the juices in the crab. Dressed crabs should be used as soon as possible. If you must store them for a short time, cover them loosely and refrigerate immediately.

Soft crabs, either dressed or undressed, may be frozen—tightly and individually wrapped—or you may purchase them already frozen at some seafood markets. Thaw frozen crabs in the refrigerator before using. They are a reasonable substitute for fresh soft crabs.

FISH

The Chesapeake Bay offers a wealth of finfish. Some of the most common are bluefish, butterfish, croaker, dogfish, drum, flounder, fluke, mackerel, monkfish, porgy, sea bass, sea trout, shad, spot, striped bass or rockfish, tile fish, and whiting. Fishing is a popular sport as well as a large industry. The fish described below are those most prized by local inhabitants.

BLUEFISH (*Pomatomus salatrix*) spawn in the Chesapeake's warm springtime water. Their dark meat has a mild flavor, reminiscent of fresh tuna, though not as strong or oily. They are excellent smoked, as well as grilled, baked, or sautéed.

ROCKFISH (*Morone saxatilis*), also known as striped bass, or striper, is the tastiest fish in the Chesapeake Bay, with firm white meat and sweet flavor. A combination of environmental factors, including pollution and increasing water temperature, as well as overfishing have depleted the rockfish population, leading to the present moratorium on the fish. Fishermen, citizens, and governments are now working together to protect the striped bass and repopulate the bay with it. Sea bass, white bass, or black bass currently may be used in place of rockfish.

SHAD (*Alosa sapidissima*), whose home waters are near the Chesapeake, has long been valued by gourmets for its flesh and its roe. The fish itself is extremely perishable, and therefore seldom shipped to other parts of the country. The roe is more widely available, and is appealing to any roe/caviar lover. It is sold in pairs, attached by a membrane that must be carefully removed before cooking. The classic roe preparation involves frying bacon to crispness, then gently sautéeing the roe sacs in the bacon fat. The bacon and roe are served together, piping hot.

OYSTERS

The Chesapeake oyster (*Crassostrea virginica*) is known to oyster lovers worldwide as one of the finest. Oysters of this species are also taken from the shallow waters of Chincoteague Bay, on the Atlantic side of the Delmarva Peninsula, and are preferred by some people for their pronounced tangy, salty flavor. Chesapeake natives eat oysters in the "R" months—September through April—because the oysters have better flavor then. Oysters may be obtained all year, however, and are carefully monitored to assure they are free of organisms harmful to humans. Although most natives prefer to eat oysters raw, they also fry, stew, steam, bake, or broil them, and use them in stuffings.

Oysters are available live in the shell, shucked, frozen, and canned. Be sure that live oysters have tightly closed shells. A general rule for oysters and other bivalves is to eat them raw only if the shells are tightly closed, and to eat them cooked only if the shells open. Shucked oysters are available in pint or quart jars, and in two grades: standard and select. The smaller standards are best for most uses. Selects are very large, good for dishes that use chopped oysters. Live and shucked oysters are perishable. Store live oysters flat on a tray and loosely covered with a dampened tea towel in the refrigerator for a day. Buy shucked oysters in sealed containers and store them in the refrigerator for up to three days; use them immediately after the seal has been broken.

The method we prefer for shucking oysters provides hand protection by using an oven mitt and a towel on which to place the oysters. Oyster shells are sharp, and the oyster knife must sometimes be used with force. Scrub the oysters well before shucking, then place an oyster on the towel so that the rounded shell is resting on the towel and the flatter shell is on top. This helps contain the juices. Next find the hinge at the narrow end of the oyster; the hinge may curve back under the bottom shell. Holding the oyster firmly on the work surface with a gloved hand, angle the oyster knife into the hinge and apply pressure. After the hinge pops, run the knife just under the top shell to the wide end of the oyster, completely freeing the shell.

Make sure that no bits of shell or mud are clinging to the knife, then loosen the oyster from the bottom shell by running the knife under it. Pick out any bits of shell with the tip of the knife. Place shucked oysters on a bed of crushed ice or rock salt for half-shell presentation. For flavor and safety, it is best to eat oysters, raw or cooked, as soon as possible after preparing them.

CRABBING AND OYSTERING

Hard shell crabs are harvested either by scooping them from a baited trot line or by using crab traps, which are similar to lobster traps.

Donald Albright, a Chesapeake waterman, above left, shows a scoopful of the over 30 million hard blue crabs harvested annually. Freshly caught, lively hard blue crabs, above, are transferred immediately to the steamer.

Gulls, the watermen's constant companions, left, in good weather, are on the lookout for a loose piece of crab bait, commonly eels.

Watermen begin oystering in the autumn and continue through the winter months, weather permitting. Above right, a trough is in place for sorting oysters, and the waterman readies his tongs. Once a good spot is established, he sets to work, right, "tonging"—bringing the oysters up from the muddy bottom. Tommy Stanfield's years on the water have accustomed him to this demanding part of oystering. Mrs. Peggy Stanfield's job of sorting the oysters, far right, is also taxing; the shells are sharp and the oysters are heavy with mud.

PICKING HARD SHELL CRABS

1. *Spread newspaper under crabs. Have a sharp paring knife and paper towels handy.*

2. *Hold body firmly, with white underside toward you, and break off two front claws at body joint. Set the claws aside.*

3. *With your thumb or knife point, pry apron flap from underside. Discard.*

4. *Turn crab over and pry top shell loose. Discard.*

5. *Remove gelatinous stomach and intestines from center cavity.*

6. *With knife, or fingers, pull back spongy gills on each side of crab. Discard.*

7. *When gills are removed, the pearly brittle inner membrane of the crab is exposed.*

8. *Snap feeler legs from the body; these can be eaten, although they have little meat.*

9. *Keep crab in one piece, as shown here, or hold at sides and break apart at center. Slice through center of the brittle membrane on each side.*

10. *Under membranes is the most succulent meat. Pry it loose with knife tip or fingers. The yellow crab mustard, or butter, has a custardy consistency and is delicious.*

11. *To remove claw meat, crack claws with the knife or crab mallet on soft white or pale pink underside.*

12. *Pull the meat loose in one piece.*

DRESSING SOFT SHELL CRABS

1. Soft shell crabs should be dressed over a sink. Be sure the crabs are alive; discard any that are not moving. Grasp the live crab in your hand.

2. Rinse the crab with cold water.

3. With a sharp pair of scissors, quickly and firmly remove the crab's face, just behind the eyes.

4. Turn the crab over and remove the apron.

5. To remove the gills, first lift the soft, hinged shells on each side of the crab.

6. The gills are easily removed with a scissors. Rinse the underside of the crab and replace shells in their original position. The crab is now ready to cook.

CRAB
FEAST

MENU

Steamed Crabs (page 119)

Roast Clams or Oysters

Barbecued Spareribs

**Cabbage Slaw with
Horseradish**

Sliced Tomatoes and Onions

Old-Fashioned Potato Salad

Roast Corn on the Cob

Blueberry Muffins

Skillet Peach Cake

Ice-Cold Watermelon

Beer and Ice Tea

Summer crab feasts are seasonal celebrations of Chesapeake life and food. They may take place at the shore or inland, but they are always casual and exuberant gatherings of friends and family.

The shores of the Chesapeake are punctuated by numerous freshwater and estuarine rivers, such as the Severn, where we held this crab feast at Little Round Bay. Many of the waterfronts are part of residential neighborhoods, with beaches, picnic areas, boat slips or moorings, and piers. Little Round Bay has the added charm of a pavilion and shade trees.

Steamed crab was the main feature at our feast; the rest of the menu followed the custom of providing ample quantities of a variety of dishes. The roast corn is a simple treat for those occasions when the grill is in operation. To roast the corn, carefully pull down the husks and remove the silk. Dip the corn in water and pull the husks back up around the corn. Place the corn on the hot grill for about 20 minutes, turning it occasionally. You may need to sprinkle the corn with a little water if it blackens too quickly.

ROAST CLAMS OR OYSTERS

As beach or backyard food, this dish provides the elemental satisfaction of all open-fire, open-air foods. Real fans eat the roasted clams or oysters plain, as soon as they are cool enough to handle, but Fresh Tomato Relish is very good with clams and Mrs. Besson's Chili Sauce suits the oysters quite well.

You can make a rack to use as a roaster, or you can use the grill rack from your barbecue. A homemade rack is preferable, because the mesh holds the clams or oysters better than the parallel bars of a grill rack, and it holds more of them.

To make the roaster, you will need two 2 x 4's, each about 6 feet long, preferably of redwood or other fire-resistant wood. You will also need a 3-foot-square piece of ¼-inch strong wire mesh. Cut 2 feet from each length of wood and place them horizontally between the remaining lengths to serve as crosspieces. Nail the crosspieces in place. Nail or staple the mesh to the crosspieces and over the long pieces to form a litter for the clams. Trim the extra wire.

You will need bricks or stones to support the roaster and a good amount of wood that burns hot with a clear flame. The actual fire pit may be constructed in various ways, as described below.

SERVES 6 TO 8

3 dozen large clams or oysters (This is a conservative estimate; people tend to be gluttonous with these.)

GARNISH (optional): Fresh Tomato Relish (page 172) or Mrs. Besson's Chili Sauce (page 171)

At the beach, dig a pit in the sand, about 2 feet deep and the width and length of the roaster. Line the perimeter of the pit with 12 bricks, or with stones wide enough to support the wood cradle of the roaster. Build a nice wood fire, one with a bright, clear flame, in the pit about 4 inches from the mesh litter. Place the clams or oysters on the mesh and keep feeding the fire until the shellfish pop open, usually in about 10 minutes.

To build a pit in the backyard, you will need 24 bricks. Place 12 bricks together in a rectangle so that the larger surfaces of the bricks form the bed of the fire pit. Line the outside perimeter of the rectangle with 12 more bricks standing on edge. The wood cradle of the roaster fits on the outside bricks, and the mesh is centered over the pit. Build a bright, clear fire with small pieces of wood and roast the clams or oysters as described above.

As the shellfish open, transfer them to a platter with tongs and send word that they are hot.

BARBECUED SPARERIBS

———

Those who profess not to like ribs become converts after tasting this recipe. There is enough sauce here for an extra pound of ribs. To serve more people, double the entire recipe and bake the ribs in two pans.

SERVES 4, OR 3 REAL RIB-EATERS

3 pounds baby backrib pork spareribs
½ cup boiling water

SAUCE

2 cups homemade Chili Sauce (page 65)
2 teaspoons Tabasco, or to taste
1 teaspoon Worcestershire sauce
2 tablespoons vinegar or lemon juice, or to taste
½ teaspoon salt
2 bay leaves

Preheat the oven to 500°. Put the ribs in a shallow baking or roasting pan large enough to hold them in one layer. Add the boiling water. Cover the ribs loosely with foil and cook for 15 minutes. Reduce the heat to 425°, remove the foil, turn the ribs, and cook for 15 minutes. Place the ribs on a rack after you take them from the oven.

Meanwhile, mix the sauce ingredients in a saucepan and bring to a simmer. Barely simmer for about 30 minutes, stirring occasionally. If there are any pan juices from the ribs, add them to the sauce and simmer another few minutes.

The ribs and sauce may be prepared ahead to this point and stored in the refrigerator. Bring the ribs and sauce to cool room temperature before grilling the ribs.

Cook the ribs over a medium-slow wood-charcoal or wood fire. Turn and baste them several times with the sauce. If desired, add about 1 cup soaked wood chips to the fire to give a smoked flavor. The ribs should be done in about 35 minutes. Perfectly cooked ribs will be succulent and have a burnished mahogany color. Cut into them if you want to test for doneness.

Skillet Peach Cake, above, is the perfect ending for a crab feast, or any summer's picnic.

Potato salad, left, is everybody's favorite down to the smallest guest.

Tangy, crunchy Cabbage Slaw, above, is a cool complement to the hot spicy crabs.

The clam-oyster rack, below, is a simple but necessary piece of equipment for roasting the bivalves.

OLD-FASHIONED POTATO SALAD

Donny Hinkleman, Susan's sister, is always asked to bring the potato salad to family gatherings or other parties. This is a variation of her recipe.

SERVES 4 TO 6; THE RECIPE MAY BE EASILY DOUBLED OR TRIPLED

1½ pounds new potatoes, scrubbed and cut into bite-size pieces

VINAIGRETTE

  2 tablespoons olive oil
  1 tablespoon white wine vinegar
  2 teaspoons fresh chopped basil, or ½ teaspoon dried basil, crumbled
  ½ teaspoon fresh chopped thyme, or ¼ teaspoon dried thyme, crumbled
  ½ teaspoon salt
    Freshly ground black pepper

  1 large celery rib, diced
  ¼ cup diced onion
  1 small sweet green pepper, diced (optional)
  2 hard-cooked eggs, diced
  ½ cup Homemade Mayonnaise (page 174)
  1 teaspoon sugar, or to taste
    Salt and freshly ground black pepper

Steam or boil the potatoes just until tender. Drain and let cool slightly. Mix the vinaigrette ingredients together in a small bowl. Place the potatoes in a bowl and pour the vinaigrette over them.

Add the diced vegetables and toss gently. Add the eggs, mayonnaise, and sugar. Season the salad with salt and pepper and toss gently. Refrigerate for at least an hour before serving; adjust the seasonings just before serving.

CABBAGE SLAW

Slaws are perennial Chesapeake salads: in mid-summer made with the season's first fresh pale green cabbage. Of the many variations, the following two are especially fine.

SERVES 6 TO 8

WITH HORSERADISH AND MAYONNAISE

  1 medium head cabbage, shredded (approximately 8 cups)
  1 medium carrot, grated
  3 tablespoons grated onion
  3 to 4 tablespoons prepared horseradish, or 2 to 3 tablespoons freshly grated horseradish
  ⅓ cup mayonnaise
  ⅓ cup sour cream
  2 teaspoons Dijon-style mustard
  ¼ teaspoon freshly ground celery seed
    Salt and freshly ground black pepper

Combine the cabbage, carrot, and onion in a bowl and toss well. Add the remaining ingredients and toss again. Taste for seasoning.

The slaw is best if prepared and refrigerated at least an hour before serving. Serve at room temperature.

WITH APPLE CIDER VINEGAR

  1 small head cabbage, shredded (about 6 cups)
  1 medium sweet red, white, or yellow onion
  1 medium green pepper
  2 medium carrots
  ½ cup olive oil or salad oil
  4 or 5 tablespoons apple cider vinegar
  1 teaspoon celery seed
    Salt and freshly ground black pepper
  ¼ cup chopped or snipped dill leaves (optional)

Place the cabbage in a large bowl. Halve the onion and green pepper and slice them very thin. Grate the carrots. Toss the vegetables with the cabbage.

Mix the oil, vinegar, and celery seed together. Season well with salt and pepper. Toss the dressing with the vegetables, and the dill if desired.

Refrigerate the slaw at least an hour before serving. Taste for seasoning and serve at room temperature.

BLUEBERRY MUFFINS

MAKES 1 DOZEN MUFFINS

1½ cups unbleached white flour
⅔ cup whole wheat pastry flour
2 teaspoons baking powder
½ teaspoon salt
¼ cup sugar
¼ teaspoon cinnamon
   Few dashes of grated nutmeg
¼ cup unsalted butter, melted
1 cup milk
2 extra large eggs
¼ teaspoon pure vanilla extract
1 cup rinsed and sorted blueberries
   Cinnamon sugar for sprinkling (1 teaspoon cinnamon mixed with 1 teaspoon sugar)

Preheat the oven to 400°. Generously butter a muffin tin. Combine the flours, baking powder, salt, sugar, and spices in a large bowl.

Mix the melted butter, milk, eggs, and vanilla in another bowl with a fork. Toss the blueberries with the flour mixture. Add the liquid ingredients to the flour mixture and stir with a fork just until blended, about 20 strokes. Do not overmix or the muffins will not be light.

Spoon the batter evenly into the buttered muffin tin, filling each cup. Sprinkle with cinnamon sugar. Bake approximately 22 minutes, or until the tops are golden brown. Cool about 5 minutes in the pan so that the muffins will be easier to remove.

SKILLET PEACH CAKE

SERVES 8 TO 10

4 tablespoons unsalted butter
½ cup dark brown sugar, packed
3 medium-large peaches, peeled and sliced
3 extra large eggs, separated
2 extra large eggs, left whole
1 cup sugar
1¼ cups unbleached white flour, sifted
4 tablespoons unsalted butter, melted and cooled
1 teaspoon pure vanilla extract
   Zest of 1 lemon
2 or 3 tablespoons dark rum (optional)

GARNISH (optional): freshly whipped cream

Melt 4 tablespoons butter over medium-low heat in a 10-inch skillet with an ovenproof handle. Add the brown sugar and stir well for 2 or 3 minutes to melt the sugar. Remove the pan from the heat. Arrange the peach slices in the bottom of the pan. Preheat the oven to 350°.

Beat 3 egg yolks with 2 whole eggs and the sugar until the mixture is a pale lemon color and very fluffy. Fold the flour into the mixture in three parts, alternating with the melted and cooled butter in two parts. Fold in the vanilla and lemon zest.

Beat the egg whites until stiff but not dry. Fold gently into the batter in three parts. Pour the batter carefully over the peach slices.

Bake the cake for about 35 minutes, or until a tester comes out clean. Remove the cake from the oven, let it stand for a few minutes, then turn it out onto a serving platter while still hot. Let the skillet rest over the platter for about 5 minutes, so that all the topping is absorbed by the cake.

Serve the cake warm, or let it cool to room temperature. If desired, drizzle 2 or 3 tablespoons of dark rum over the cake. Serve whipped cream with the cake, if you like.

—

BOAT
LUNCH

—

MENU

Soft Crab Sandwiches

Potato Salad with Radish
and Scallion Vinaigrette

Mema's Sugar Cookies
with Cherry Jelly

Ginger Nuts

Fresh Cherries or Plums

Beer, Soft Drinks,
and Deviled Tomato Juice

We were pleased to have this lunch under sail aboard the *Jeanne,* a wooden boat designed and built by the Cutts & Case Boatyard of Oxford, Maryland. Handmade wooden vessels are a rarity these days, especially those like the *Jeanne*—one-of-a-kind and skillfully crafted by knowledgeable boatbuilders. Ed Cutts, Jr., deftly skippered us out the Tred Avon River on a bright, crisp sailing day. Like many of the natives, we think this approach to the Bay from Oxford is one of the finest sails in the region.

Boat meals should be easy to prepare and serve. This menu was designed to satisfy water-whetted appetites and to be eaten both with a fork and out-of-hand. To make the Deviled Tomato Juice, we use home-canned or commercial juice and spice it with Chesapeake seafood seasoning to taste.

SOFT CRAB SANDWICHES

Of the many ways to serve soft crabs, sandwiches are very popular and traditional. The crabs are often deep-fried, especially in restaurants. We prefer pan-fried soft crabs, because their flavor seems more delicate. Directions for dressing crabs are on page 25.

SERVES 4

- 4 large soft crabs
  Salt and freshly ground black pepper
- 6 tablespoons butter or oil
- 1 egg, lightly beaten
- ½ cup all-purpose flour
- 4 round rolls, such as Kaiser rolls
  Sliced tomato
  Lettuce
  Sliced onion
  Mayonnaise

Dress the crabs and sprinkle them lightly with salt and pepper. Heat the butter or oil over medium heat in a pan large enough to hold the crabs in one layer, or fry them in two batches, if necessary. Dip the crabs in the beaten egg, then dredge lightly with flour. Put them in the pan immediately, belly side down.

Fry until they are golden red-brown and the back feeler legs are crisp, 5 or 6 minutes on each side.

Arrange the rolls, tomato, lettuce, and onion on a platter so that each person can make a sandwich. Serve with plain mayonnaise or season the mayonnaise with Chesapeake seafood seasoning to taste. Or serve the sandwiches already assembled.

POTATO SALAD WITH RADISH AND SCALLION VINAIGRETTE

SERVES 4 TO 8

- 2 pounds small white potatoes
- ½ cup olive oil
- 1 bunch scallions, trimmed to 3 inches of green and sliced thin
- 6 to 8 radishes, sliced thin
- ¼ cup white wine vinegar
  Pinch of sugar
  Salt and freshly ground black pepper
- ¼ cup chopped parsley or mixed fresh herbs

Scrub the potatoes and cook them in their jackets just until done. Keep warm.

Heat 2 tablespoons of the oil over medium heat. Sauté the scallions and radishes for 1 or 2 minutes. Add the vinegar, the remaining oil, and the sugar. Season well with salt and pepper.

Peel and slice the potatoes.

Warm the dressing thoroughly, then pour it over the warm sliced potatoes. Add the parsley or herbs and toss. Serve warm or at room temperature.

MEMA'S SUGAR COOKIES WITH CHERRY JELLY

APPROXIMATELY 8 DOZEN COOKIE-PRESS COOKIES, OR 6 DOZEN SLICED COOKIES

½ pound unsalted butter, softened
¼ pound margarine, softened
1½ cups sugar
3 extra large eggs
1½ teaspoons pure vanilla extract
4 cups unbleached white flour
2 teaspoons baking powder
½ teaspoon salt
Approximately ⅓ cup cherry jelly

Cream the butter and margarine well. Add the sugar and cream well. Add the eggs and beat them into the batter for 1 minute. Add the vanilla and stir well.

Sift the flour, baking powder, and salt together. Add to the egg mixture in batches, blending well after each addition.

If you are making the pressed cookies, preheat the oven to 350°.

Fill a cookie press and press cookies onto ungreased baking sheets 1 inch apart. Make a small indentation in the center of each cookie with the tip of a spoon. Fill with about ⅛ teaspoon cherry jelly.

Alternately, place the dough on plastic wrap and roll it into 5 or 6 cylinders about 2 inches wide. Refrigerate for at least an hour. Preheat the oven to 350°. Slice the dough about ¼ inch thick and prepare with jelly as directed for pressed cookies.

Bake the cookies in batches for 12 to 15 minutes, until the tops are pale golden brown and the bottoms are medium golden brown. Change the position of the baking sheets about halfway through baking. Cool the cookies on racks and store in airtight cookie tins.

GINGER NUTS

This recipe has been adapted from one in Fifty Years in a Maryland Kitchen *by Mrs. B. C. Howard.*

MAKES APPROXIMATELY 4 DOZEN

¾ cup unbleached white flour
1 teaspoon powdered ginger
½ teaspoon salt
½ cup brown sugar
⅓ cup unsalted butter
⅓ cup dark molasses
2 tablespoons finely chopped crystallized ginger

Preheat the oven to 350°. Generously butter three large baking sheets or cookie sheets and line with parchment paper.

Sift the flour with the ginger and salt.

Put the sugar, butter, and molasses in a saucepan over low heat. Stir constantly to dissolve the sugar and melt the butter. Do not allow the mixture to boil. Remove from the heat. Stir in the flour mixture and the chopped ginger.

Using 2 teaspoons, drop the mixture, about 1 teaspoon for each cookie, 2 inches apart onto the prepared baking sheets.

Bake the cookies for 8 to 10 minutes, changing the position of the sheets halfway through the baking. The cookies are done when the bottoms are medium brown and the tops are bubbling. Leave the cookies on the parchment and transfer to racks. When the cookies are cool, remove from parchment and store in airtight cookie tins lined with wax paper.

—

HOLIDAY DINNER

—

MENU

Warm Goose Salad

Oyster Chowder

Squash Puff in Baked Onions

Beets with Crème Fraîche and
Horseradish

Southern Maryland Stuffed
Ham

Leeks and Turnips

Mrs. Ridgely's Dinner Rolls

Cranberry Chutney

Alma's Coconut Cake

Poached Winter Fruit with
Persimmon Cream

Maryland White and Red
Wines

O ur holiday dinner took place at the mid-nine-teenth-century home of Dr. and Mrs. John Martielli in Ellicott City, Maryland. We joined the Martielli family and their friends in the formal dining room, a lovely setting with its original fireplace and marble mantelpiece and collection of family silver, china, and furniture. A crackling fire provided additional warmth and cheer to the occasion.

Following our preference for complementing menus with local wines, we selected Maryland vintages for this dinner. If you cannot find these wines, serve Chardonnay or Sauvignon Blanc and Cabernet Sauvignon. This menu, which is appropriate for Thanksgiving, Christmas, New Year's Day, or any winter celebration, offers both traditional and modern dishes. The soup, ham, squash puff, rolls, and cake are our versions of some time-honored Chesapeake recipes. The other dishes feature regional ingredients in contemporary recipes.

WARM GOOSE SALAD

If you're far from fields full of wild geese or mushrooms, this salad is also tasty made with commercial duck breasts or cultivated mushrooms.

SERVES 10 TO 12

½ pound chanterelle mushrooms
4 whole Canada goose breasts
½ cup olive oil, approximately
4 shallots, sliced very thin
Salt and freshly ground black pepper
3 or 4 tablespoons Raspberry Vinegar (page 173)
3 quarts cleaned winter salad greens, such as watercress, curly endive, and escarole, approximately

Clean the mushrooms with a brush or a damp towel. Trim the stems and slice the mushrooms about ¼ inch thick.

Sauté the goose breasts in 2 tablespoons of the oil over medium-high heat. Turn to brown evenly and cook just until medium rare, about 6 minutes. Transfer to a plate and keep warm.

Add a little oil to the pan and sauté the mushrooms and shallots for a few minutes, until crisp-tender. Remove them to the plate with the goose. Slice the goose breasts on the diagonal about ¼ inch thick. Season the goose and mushrooms with salt and pepper to taste and keep warm.

Add the raspberry vinegar to the pan and deglaze the pan over medium-high heat for a minute. Stir in the rest of the oil and heat briefly.

Arrange the salad greens on a serving platter. Toss the goose and mushrooms with the dressing and arrange on top of the greens. Serve immediately.

OYSTER CHOWDER

This is a variation of a popular Chesapeake chowder. Many people fry a couple of bacon slices and use the fat in place of the butter, then crumble the bacon to garnish the soup. We think the oyster flavor is better without the bacon. This recipe may be easily doubled to serve more.

SERVES 4 TO 6

1 pint standard shucked oysters, or 2 dozen
   oysters in the shell
2 tablespoons unsalted butter
1 small onion, diced
2 fresh thyme sprigs, or ½ teaspoon dried thyme
1 medium potato, about 6 ounces, peeled and
   diced
2 cups milk
1 cup half-and-half
   Salt and freshly ground pepper

GARNISH: a few chopped parsley leaves
           oyster crackers

Remove any bits of shell and the muscles from the
shucked oysters. Strain and reserve the liquor. Or
shuck the oysters in the shell (page 21), remove any
bits of shell, and save the liquor.

Melt the butter over low heat in a soup pot. Add
the diced onion and cook until softened, about 10
minutes. Add the thyme, potato, milk, half-and-half,
and the reserved oyster liquor. Cook at a bare simmer
until the potatoes are just done, about 6 minutes. Add
the oysters and cook just until their edges curl, about
3 minutes. Adjust the seasoning with salt and pepper.
Serve hot, garnished with the chopped parsley or oyster crackers.

SQUASH PUFF IN BAKED ONIONS

SERVES 10 TO 12

12 small yellow onions, about 3½ pounds
   Salt and freshly ground black pepper
 2 extra large eggs, separated
¼ cup half-and-half
 2 cups mashed or pureed cooked winter
   squash: butternut or acorn; mashed or
   pureed sweet potato also works well

GARNISH: chopped parsley or chervil

Peel the onions, but leave as much of the stem and
root ends as possible. Parboil in lightly salted boiling
water for about 10 minutes. Drain and let cool.

Slice off one-third of each onion from the stem
end. Reserve for another use. Cut thin slices from the
root ends to allow the onions to stand in a baking
dish. Remove all but 2 layers of the onions from the
centers. Salt and pepper the cases lightly. Place the

onions in a generously buttered baking dish just large
enough to hold them in 1 layer. This may be done
up to 8 hours ahead, and the onions covered with a
damp towel and refrigerated.

About 30 minutes before serving, beat the egg
yolks lightly with the half-and-half. Stir the mixture
into the squash puree and season well with salt and
pepper. Preheat the oven to 400°.

Beat the egg whites until stiff but not dry. Fold
the whites into the squash. Spoon the mixture onto
the onions, not packing it, but heaping lightly. Place
any remaining mixture between the onions.

Bake on the lowest oven shelf for 20 to 25 minutes, until the squash is puffed and lightly browned.
Garnish with chopped parsley or chervil and serve
hot.

BEETS WITH CRÈME FRAÎCHE
AND HORSERADISH

SERVES 10 TO 12

2½ pounds small beets
1½ cups crème fraîche
 ½ cup freshly grated horseradish
   Salt and pepper
 ½ cup fine dry breadcrumbs

Trim the beet roots and stems to about 1 inch. Place
the beets in a pot with enough water to cover, and
boil until almost tender, about 20 minutes. Drain and
refresh under cold water; peel and slice about ¼ inch
thick.

Preheat the oven to 350°. Mix the crème fraîche
with the horseradish. Season to taste with salt and
pepper. Pour a little of the mixture into a shallow
baking dish just large enough to hold the beets. Add
half of the beet slices. Pour half of the crème fraîche
over the beets. Repeat with the rest of the beets and
the remaining crème fraîche.

Bake for 20 minutes. Sprinkle with the breadcrumbs and bake for an additional 10 to 15 minutes,
until the crumbs are lightly browned. Serve hot.

Oyster Chowder, above, is a typical Chesapeake dish—simple and very satisfying.

A salad of Canada goose breast and chanterelle mushrooms, above right, opens the menu of seasonal regional specialties.

Southern Maryland Stuffed Ham, traditionally served at Christmas, New Year's, and Easter, is complemented by Squash Puff in Baked Onions and Beets with Crème Fraîche and Horseradish, left and right.

SOUTHERN MARYLAND
STUFFED HAM

Corned hams have a special flavor; they are put into the corning liquid fresh, and are quite perishable. Consequently, they are difficult to find outside the region. Fresh hams, those that have not been long-cured or smoked, or even lightly cured hams, may be substituted. It is well worth searching out and stuffing the right ham. This very old dish, of which there are many slight variations, is traditionally served at Christmas and Easter. The ham should be made at least one day ahead, and may be, to good effect, cooked three or four days ahead. It keeps well in the refrigerator for about a week if tightly wrapped. It can also be sliced, packed in ½-pound or smaller packages, and frozen for up to 3 months.

SERVES 10 TO 16

```
 1  10- to 12-pound corned ham, or other lightly
    cured ham
 3  pounds kale
 3  pounds cabbage
 2  pounds yellow onions
 1  pound scallions
 2  tablespoons celery seed
 2  tablespoons mustard seed
1½  tablespoons salt
 1  tablespoon freshly ground black pepper
 ¼  cup cayenne, or more to taste
```

Trim the ham of rind and most of the fat. Chop the kale—leaves and tender stems only—into small pieces. Chop the cabbage into small pieces. Blanch the kale and cabbage in abundant boiling water for 5 minutes. Refresh under cold running water and drain in a colander set over a large bowl. Press well, but do not squeeze, to extract excess liquid. Reserve the liquid.

Peel and trim the yellow onions and fine-dice them. Trim the scallions, leaving about 6 inches of green, and slice them crosswise. Mix all the vegetables together in a large bowl. Add the celery seed, mustard seed, salt, black pepper, and cayenne. Some people add more cayenne—as one cook puts it, "until the hands begin to burn slightly while mixing."

Make deep slits in the ham with a thin, narrow knife. The cuts should be made perpendicular to the bone, so that the ham shows a nice pattern when it is sliced. Pack the ham with the stuffing, pushing it into each cut to pack as fully as possible. Cover the ham with the remaining stuffing. This procedure is messy; it helps to work next to the sink.

To cook, wrap the ham securely in a large piece of tightly woven professional-grade cheesecloth. Many people reserve an old pillowcase to enclose the ham. If you use a pillowcase, be sure there are no air pockets in it. The ham should be tightly wrapped and tied with a strong piece of kitchen twine. You will need twine about three and one-half times the length of the ham. Any twine can be used as long as it is made from fiber, preferably cotton, and not nylon or plastic.

Place a rack (a 9 or 10-inch inverted pie tin may be used for this) in a large noncorrodible pot to prevent the ham from sticking to the bottom. Lower the ham into the pot, then add the reserved vegetable liquor and hot water to cover. Bring to a boil, reduce the heat to a simmer, cover the pot, and cook for 20 minutes per pound.

Cool the ham in its liquor. Remove the ham and wrap it well with foil, then refrigerate. Remove from the refrigerator about 2 hours before serving. To serve, slice the ham thinly from the top down toward the bone to show the stuffing. The pot liquor is good for seasoning vegetables, or as a stock for ham-based soups such as bean or split pea, or for soups made with fresh peas or other green vegetables. Store the pot liquor in the freezer in convenient-size containers; it will keep frozen for about 6 months.

LEEKS AND TURNIPS

Either heavy cream or half-and-half can be used here. Our choice depends on our mood for a farmhouse rich vegetable dish and on what else we are serving.

SERVES 4 TO 6

```
1¼ to 1½ pounds small turnips
 1  to 1¼ pounds leeks
 2  tablespoons unsalted butter
 ½  teaspoon fresh chopped marjoram, or
    ¼ teaspoon dried marjoram
    Freshly grated nutmeg
    Salt and freshly ground black pepper
 ½  to ¾ cup heavy cream or half-and-half
 ⅓  cup fine dry breadcrumbs
```

Scrub the turnips and peel them if the skins are tough. Cut the turnips in half, then in ¼-inch slices. Pan-steam in a little water 3 to 5 minutes, just until crisp-tender. Drain and set aside.

Trim and wash the leeks well. Leave some of the pale tender green stem. Cut the leeks into ¼-inch rounds. Pan-steam in a little water 3 or 4 minutes, just until crisp-tender. Drain and set aside.

Preheat oven to 375°. Butter a 1- or 1½-quart baking dish with 1 tablespoon of butter.

Spread the turnips in the dish. Scatter half of the fresh marjoram over the turnips, or crumble half of the dried marjoram. Season lightly with nutmeg, salt, and pepper.

Spread the leeks over the turnips and scatter or crumble the remaining marjoram. Season lightly with nutmeg, salt, and pepper. Pour the cream over the dish, using the larger quantity if you used the larger quantity of vegetables. Sprinkle the breadcrumbs on top.

Bake for 25 to 30 minutes, until the top is lightly browned. Serve hot.

MRS. RIDGELY'S DINNER ROLLS

Marguerite Riggs Ridgely was famous for these rolls, which she served for special occasions and at family gatherings.

MAKES 3 DOZEN 3-INCH ROLLS

2 tablespoons active dry yeast
½ cup warm water
½ teaspoon sugar plus 1 scant tablespoon
2 cups milk
1 cup vegetable shortening
1 teaspoon salt
2 extra large eggs
1 extra large egg white
8 cups unbleached white flour
4 tablespoons unsalted butter, melted

Combine the yeast, water, and ½ teaspoon of the sugar in a small bowl and let stand until foamy.

Scald the milk. Add the shortening, salt, and remaining sugar to a large mixing bowl. Pour the hot milk over the shortening and stir until the shortening is dissolved.

Beat the eggs and egg white in a small bowl with a fork. Slowly add about ½ cup of the hot milk mixture to the eggs, beating well with a fork. Slowly beat the egg mixture into the hot milk mixture.

Add 4 cups of the flour to the milk mixture, 1 cup at a time, stirring well with a wooden spoon after each addition. Add the yeast mixture and 1 cup of flour and blend well. Add another cup of flour, blend well, and scrape down sides of bowl. Cover the bowl with a damp tea towel and let the sponge rise in a warm place for 1 hour, until almost doubled in bulk. Punch down the dough and turn it onto a lightly floured board. Add the remaining 2 cups of flour, ½ cup at a time, kneading it in after each addition. Knead for about 10 minutes.

Transfer the dough to a lightly oiled bowl, cover with a damp tea towel, and let the dough rise for 1 hour, until almost doubled in bulk. (This rising may be done in the refrigerator overnight. Bring the dough to cool room temperature before shaping it.) Punch down the dough and shape into rolls.

Use the 4 tablespoons of melted butter to grease baking pans and to brush on top of each roll.

The rolls may be shaped in a variety of ways. Mrs. Ridgely usually made Parker House rolls. These are made by gently rolling the dough ½ inch thick and cutting it into rounds with a 2½-inch cutter. Fold the rounds almost in half, and place them on lightly buttered baking sheets.

Cloverleaf rolls are made by pulling off bits of dough and rolling them into balls about 1 inch in diameter. Place 3 balls in each cup of a lightly buttered muffin tin.

To make fan-shaped rolls, gently roll the dough about ⅜ inch thick, then cut into 1½-inch squares. For each roll, stack 4 squares and place each stack vertically in the cup of a buttered muffin tin.

Brush the tops of the rolls with the melted butter.

Preheat the oven to 375°. Place the rolls in a warm spot to rise until almost doubled in bulk, about 20 minutes. Bake the rolls for about 25 minutes, until golden brown on top. Change the position of the pans on the racks halfway through the baking time to ensure the rolls are baked evenly.

John Martielli, left, gathers firewood for the dining room hearth.

Mrs. Ridgely's Dinner Rolls stay warm, right, in a hand-embroidered linen roll server.

Alma's Coconut Cake, below, is a treasured recipe from Claire Martielli's mother, Alma Belsinger. Poached Winter Fruit with Persimmon Cream is garnished with caramel.

CRANBERRY CHUTNEY

The lively taste of this chutney goes well with game, beef, pork, or poultry. We also like it on toasted bagels with cream cheese.

MAKES ABOUT 6 HALF-PINTS

- 2 cups water
- ¼ cup red wine vinegar
- 1 tablespoon plus 1 teaspoon coriander seeds
- 20 allspice berries
- 8 ⅛-inch-thick slices of fresh peeled ginger
- 24 black peppercorns
- 1½ pounds cranberries, rinsed and sorted
- 2 large onions (about 1 pound), peeled and chopped
- 2 firm ripe pears (about 14 ounces), peeled, cored, and chopped
- 2 large garlic cloves, minced fine
- 1 hot red pepper, seeds removed and chopped fine (optional)
- 1½ cups sugar
- 1½ teaspoons salt

Combine the water and vinegar in a noncorrodible saucepan. Add the coriander, allspice, ginger, and peppercorns. Bring the mixture to a boil and simmer for 10 minutes.

Combine the rest of the ingredients in a large, heavy noncorrodible pan. Strain the spice liquid over the cranberry mixture.

Bring to a boil. Reduce the heat and simmer for about 35 minutes, stirring occasionally. Ladle into hot, sterilized half-pint jars, leaving ¼-inch head space. Seal and process in a boiling water bath for 10 minutes. Remove the jars from the water, cover with a towel, and let cool to room temperature. Check the seals; store unsealed jars in the refrigerator and use as soon as possible.

ALMA'S COCONUT CAKE

Fresh coconut gives this cake its fine flavor. For the required quantities of liquid and shredded coconut, choose a coconut weighing about two pounds. Shake it to be sure that it has liquid inside. Punch holes in the coconut's "eyes" with an ice pick or a large, clean nail. Drain and reserve the liquid. To help open the coconut, place it in a preheated 350° oven for 15 minutes. After it has cooled, tap it with a hammer until it breaks into pieces. Remove the meat from the shell and remove the thin brown skin from the meat with a vegetable peeler or sharp paring knife. Shred the coconut in a food processor or with a hand grater.

SERVES 8 TO 12

- 1½ cups sugar
- 2 extra large eggs, left whole
- 3 extra large eggs, separated
- 1 teaspoon pure vanilla extract
- ½ cup fresh coconut liquid
- 2½ cups cake flour
- 2 teaspoons baking powder
- ½ teaspoon salt
- ⅛ teaspoon freshly ground nutmeg
- 12 tablespoons unsalted butter, melted and cooled
  Vanilla Buttercream Frosting
- 5 cups freshly shredded coconut

Butter and flour three 8-inch cake pans. Preheat the oven to 350°.

Beat the sugar with the 2 eggs and 3 egg yolks until the mixture is very light and fluffy. Add the vanilla and coconut liquid.

Sift the flour with the baking powder, salt, and nutmeg. Add the dry ingredients to the egg mixture in three batches, alternating with the melted butter.

Beat the egg whites until stiff. Fold gently into the batter in three batches. Pour the batter into the prepared pans and bake for about 25 minutes, or until the cakes are light golden brown and a tester comes out clean. Cool the cakes in the pans for 10 minutes, then remove and cool on racks.

When cool, spread one layer generously with frosting and cover with about 1 cup of the coconut. Add the second layer and repeat with frosting and coconut. Place the third layer on top and frost the sides. Then frost the top and cover the entire cake with the remaining coconut.

VANILLA BUTTERCREAM FROSTING

MAKES APPROXIMATELY 3 CUPS, ENOUGH TO FROST A 3-LAYER CAKE

4 cups confectioners' sugar
½ cup unsalted butter, softened
2 to 3 tablespoons heavy cream
1 teaspoon pure vanilla extract
2 tablespoons light corn syrup

Sift the confectioners' sugar. Cream the butter in a mixer. With the machine running add the sugar, ½ cup at a time. As the frosting begins to stiffen, add the cream, 1 tablespoon at a time. After half of the sugar has been added, add the vanilla. Add half of the remaining sugar, then add 1 tablespoon of corn syrup. Add the rest of the sugar and whip in the final tablespoon of corn syrup.

The frosting may be held at room temperature for up to 30 minutes if the bowl is immediately covered with a damp paper towel.

POACHED WINTER FRUIT WITH PERSIMMON CREAM

Here is an elegant company dessert that may be prepared a day ahead and assembled just before serving. If your guests include children, tell them to crunch the caramel gently, as the pieces can be sharp.

SERVES 10 TO 12

PERSIMMON CREAM

¾ pound cultivated persimmons, dead ripe, or
    1¼ pounds wild persimmons, dead ripe
    Few drops of lemon juice
1 cup heavy cream
⅓ to ½ cup sugar
2 egg yolks

POACHED FRUIT

1 whole fresh pineapple, 2½ to 3 pounds
3 navel oranges, approximately 1¼ pounds,
    or 6 seedless mandarins or tangerines
2 cups water
½ cup sugar

CARAMEL

¼ cup water
1 cup sugar

Peel, seed, and puree the persimmons. Stir in a few drops of lemon juice.

Heat the cream. Add ⅓ cup sugar if you are using cultivated persimmons, or ½ cup sugar if you are using wild persimmons. Stir the sugar to dissolve it. Beat the egg yolks lightly; add a little hot cream to them. Add the yolk mixture to the remaining cream, stirring constantly. Cook over very low heat, still stirring constantly, until the mixture coats a spoon, about 10 minutes.

Remove the custard from the heat, cover, and cool to room temperature. Stir in the persimmon puree. Add a few drops of lemon juice to adjust the taste if necessary. Lay wax paper or plastic wrap directly on the cream and refrigerate.

Meanwhile, prepare the poached fruit. Cut the rind from the pineapple, then cut the pineapple in half lengthwise. Remove the core carefully, and cut the pineapple crosswise into slices about ½ inch thick. Reserve the juice.

Peel the oranges or tangerines and separate the sections. Put the reserved pineapple juice, water, and sugar in a pan large enough to hold all of the fruit. Bring the mixture to a simmer and add the fruit. If you are using tangerines, add them about 3 minutes after the pineapple. Cover and poach the fruit just until tender, about 10 minutes.

Remove the fruit to a platter with a slotted spoon. Reserve the syrup for another use. If you are poaching the fruit a day ahead, moisten with a little syrup, cover, and refrigerate.

Oil a marble slab or two baking sheets with vegetable oil. To prepare the caramel, put the water in a saucepan and stir in the sugar. Place over medium-low heat and stir constantly until the caramel is a medium golden brown.

Remove from heat, and working quickly with a spoon, drizzle the caramel in free-form threads over the oiled marble or baking sheets. If necessary, place the pan of caramel in a shallow pan of simmering water to keep it liquid enough to drizzle.

When the caramel is cool, peel it from the oiled surface and break it into uneven pieces. You may store the caramel in an airtight cookie tin lined with wax paper for a day before assembling the dessert.

To assemble the dessert, spread the persimmon cream on a serving platter. Arrange the poached fruit on top of the cream. Refrigerate for an hour or two. Strew the caramel over the top just before serving.

STEEPLE-
CHASE
PICNIC

S teeplechases are long-standing annual springtime events in the Chesapeake region, where they attract thousands of viewers. A steeplechase is a single race, usually with six or seven horses entered. The Maryland Hunt Cup is the best known and most arduous of the several chases run in Maryland and Virginia. Rolling green countryside near Monkton, Maryland, is the setting for this race, which has a course four miles long with five 5-foot-high fences. The horses take about nine minutes to run the circuit twice and complete the race.

Spectators commonly make an afternoon of the steeplechase, bringing picnics to spread on the lawn or arrange on tailgates. Menus are often elaborate, and some people even bring their best silver, crystal, and linens. We chose elegance, too—our menu is deliciously extravagant—and we arrived in style. The tailgate we set our champagne and dessert upon is actually the luggage rack of a vintage 1940 Packard Darrin Custom Super-8, One-Eighty Convertible Victoria.

Springtime in full bloom, high clouds in a blue sky, and a perfect picnic setting made a winning afternoon for all.

CHICKEN CONSOMMÉ WITH ASPARAGUS TIPS

This recipe uses clarified broth. Before clarifying, it is necessary to make the broth ahead and refrigerate it, so that the fat can be completely removed. Take out the fat (there should not be much) while the broth is cold and jellylike.

SERVES 6 TO 8

  2 quarts Rich Chicken Broth (page 108)
  2 egg whites
  2 eggshells
1¼ to 1½ pounds asparagus
    Salt and freshly ground white pepper

To clarify the broth, first let it come to room temperature in a soup pot. Beat the egg whites lightly and whisk them briefly into the broth. Crush the eggshells and stir them into the broth.

Heat the broth very slowly to just a simmer. Do not stir. Simmer, so that the bubbles are just breaking the surface, for about 20 minutes. The egg whites will coagulate into a froth containing the particulate matter in the broth. Gently push the froth aside to be sure the broth is just simmering.

Carefully remove most of the froth with a ladle. Then ladle the broth through a colander lined with rinsed, fine-weave cheesecloth. The broth may be clarified ahead of time and refrigerated until ready to use.

Trim 1½ inches of the tips from the asparagus spears. Pan-steam the tips in a little water, just until crisp-tender, 2 or 3 minutes. These may be prepared ahead of time.

Simmer the broth to reduce it a little—it should have a rich color and flavor. Season lightly with salt and white pepper. Have the consommé very hot before garnishing it with the asparagus tips. Serve immediately.

LOBSTER IN LETTUCE CUPS

SERVES 4 TO 8

⅓ cup sea salt or kosher salt
3 or 4 sprigs Italian parsley
½ lemon, sliced
2 1¼-pound lobsters
2 heads limestone or butter lettuce
2 shallots, diced
3 or 4 tarragon sprigs
5 or 6 chervil sprigs
½ cup fruity olive oil
2 tablespoons white wine vinegar
1 tablespoon lemon juice, or to taste
   Salt and freshly ground black pepper

In a pot large enough to hold the lobsters comfortably, make a court bouillon by bringing 12 quarts of water to a boil with the sea salt, parsley stems (reserve the leaves), and sliced lemon. Boil for 10 minutes, then add the lobsters and cook for 8 to 10 minutes.

Remove the lobsters from the pot and let them cool. When they are cool enough to handle, remove the meat from the tails and claws, reserving the shells, body meat, tomalley, and coral to make Lobster Bisque (page 107).

Cut the tail meat crosswise to make attractive disk-shaped pieces. Leave the meat from the claws whole if you are serving four. If you are serving eight, cut the meat in half lengthwise, beginning at the point where the pincers branch out. Cover and store in the refrigerator until ready to serve.

Clean and dry the lettuce. Choose the prettiest cup-shaped leaves, and store in the crisper.

Cut the shallots in a fine dice. Chop the leaves from the parsley, tarragon, and chervil. Put the olive oil in a bowl and whisk in the vinegar and lemon juice. Stir in the shallots and herbs. Season with salt and pepper.

To serve, bring the lettuce and lobster meat to cool room temperature. Arrange the lettuce cups in small bowls or on plates, and spoon some of the vinaigrette into each. Add a layer of lobster meat and spoon some vinaigrette over it. Repeat layers until all the lobster is used. Garnish with the claw meat.

GRILLED LEG OF LAMB WITH RASPBERRY VINEGAR

You may use commercial raspberry vinegar, but taste it first for sharpness. If it is very sharp, reduce the amount by ¼ cup. Homemade raspberry vinegar has more natural fruit flavor and sugar and less acidity. This lamb makes especially tasty sandwiches on Sweet Potato Rolls accompanied by Raspberry Mayonnaise (page 174).

SERVES 6 TO 8

1 5- to 6-pound leg of lamb
4 large garlic cloves
1 cup Raspberry Vinegar (page 173), or
   commercial brand
2 tablespoons olive oil
8 to 10 sprigs fresh thyme, or 2 teaspoons dried
   thyme
   Salt and freshly ground black pepper
   Sweet Potato Rolls

Bone and butterfly the lamb, or have your butcher do this. Remove excess fat, but leave the skin. Make slits in the meat with a small, sharp knife. Cut 2 of the garlic cloves into slivers and insert into the meat.

Place the lamb in a dish just large enough to hold it. Mix the vinegar with the oil and pour the mixture over the lamb. Rub the fresh thyme between your palms to bruise it, and add it to the marinade. Or crumble the dried thyme over the lamb. Crush the remaining garlic and scatter it over the lamb.

Marinate for 8 hours or overnight, covered, in the refrigerator. Turn the lamb three or four times during marination.

Prepare a medium-hot wood or wood-charcoal fire. Remove the lamb from the marinade and brush off the herbs. Salt and pepper the meat lightly and place it on the grill skin side down. For rare to medium-rare lamb, cook 30 to 45 minutes, turning and basting several times with the marinade.

To serve, let the lamb rest for a few minutes off the grill, then carve into ¼-inch-thick slices. To serve in sandwiches, let the lamb come to room temperature, trim away any remaining fat, and carve into slices about ⅛ inch thick.

The Maryland Hunt Cup steeplechase, left, brings viewers from all over the country.

Steeplechase fans, below, set a stylish tailgate under a dogwood in full bloom.

A picnic of grilled lamb sandwiches and lobster salad awaits the guests, right.

The horses are decked with finery, below right.

Rich Fudgy Brownies and luscious Raspberry Cupcakes are garnished with fresh violets, below far right.

SWEET POTATO ROLLS

MAKES 2 DOZEN 5-INCH ROLLS

>   1 medium sweet potato, approximately 8
>   ounces
>   3 tablespoons sugar
>   1 tablespoon active dry yeast
>   6 cups unbleached white flour
> 1½ teaspoons salt
>   1 cup milk, scalded and cooled
>   2 extra large eggs, at room temperature
>   1 tablespoon vegetable oil

Peel and chop the sweet potato coarsely. Place in a saucepan, barely cover with water, and cook until tender. Drain the cooking liquid into a measuring cup and reserve. Mash the potato while it is still hot and stir in 2 tablespoons of the sugar. Set aside to cool.

Add enough very warm water to the reserved cooking liquid to make 1 cup. Stir the remaining tablespoon of sugar and the yeast into the liquid. Let stand for about 10 minutes, or until foamy.

Measure 5½ cups of the flour into a large bowl and stir in the salt. Make a well in the flour.

Combine milk, eggs, and oil with the mashed sweet potato. Add the yeast mixture and stir until well blended. Pour into the well in the flour and incorporate the flour into the liquid to make a soft dough.

Sprinkle the remaining ½ cup flour on a work surface. Gather the dough and transfer to the floured surface. Gently knead the dough; it will be soft, but it should not be sticky. Sprinkle a little more flour over the dough if necessary.

Place the dough in a lightly oiled bowl, cover with a damp tea towel, and let it rise until doubled in bulk. This first rising may be done in the refrigerator overnight, in which case, cover the bowl tightly with plastic wrap.

Punch down the dough, and let it rise until doubled in bulk. Punch it down again and divide it in half.

Place the dough on a floured work surface and roll each portion into a cylinder about 2½ inches in diameter. Cut crosswise into generous 1-inch-thick slices. Dust each slice lightly on both sides with flour. Preheat the oven to 400°.

Place the rolls at least 1 inch apart on lightly buttered baking sheets. Cover with tea towels and let the dough rise in a warm place about 20 minutes. Bake for 20 minutes, until golden brown, changing the position of the pans halfway through the baking.

Cool the rolls on a rack before making sandwiches.

Rolls can be stored in a tightly closed container, or frozen individually and packed in freezer bags. They will keep in the freezer for 2 weeks to a month. To serve, place the frozen rolls on a baking sheet and cover tightly with foil. Bake at 350° until heated through, about 15 minutes. To accompany a meal, the rolls can be served hot from the oven.

FUDGY BROWNIES WITH MOCHA BUTTERCREAM

We like to make these brownies in a 9½-inch springform pan and serve them cut into wedges; they may also be baked in a 9- or 10-inch square pan and cut into squares.

MAKES 10 TO 12 BROWNIES

>   4 ounces unsweetened chocolate
> ½ cup unsalted butter
>   3 extra large eggs
> 1⅓ cups sugar
>   1 cup unbleached white flour
>   Scant ½ teaspoon salt
>   1 teaspoon pure vanilla extract
>   Mocha Buttercream

Preheat the oven to 350°. Generously butter a 9½-inch springform pan or a 9- or 10-inch-square baking pan.

Melt the chocolate with the butter in a heavy-bottomed pan over low heat. Remove from the heat. Beat the eggs and sugar in a bowl until the sugar is dissolved and the mixture is fluffy. Blend in the chocolate mixture. Add the flour and salt and blend well. Stir in the vanilla.

Pour the batter into the prepared pan and bake for 30 to 35 minutes, until tester comes out clean. Cool in the pan on a rack.

To frost, remove the side of the springform pan and spread Mocha Buttercream smoothly over the top of the brownies.

MOCHA BUTTERCREAM

MAKES APPROXIMATELY 1¼ CUPS, ENOUGH FOR
1 RECIPE OF BROWNIES OR A 1-LAYER CAKE

4 tablespoons unsalted butter, softened
  Approximately 1½ cups confectioners' sugar,
  sifted
1 tablespoon instant espresso powder dissolved
  in 1 tablespoon coffee or warm water

Cream the butter in a mixing bowl until fluffy. Add the confectioners' sugar, about ¼ cup at a time, blending well after each addition. About halfway through adding the sugar, add the coffee. Continue beating and adding the sugar until the frosting is a thick spreading consistency.

RASPBERRY CUPCAKES

MAKES APPROXIMATELY 24 CUPCAKES

2½ cups sifted cake flour
2½ teaspoons baking powder
 ½ teaspoon baking soda
 ⅛ teaspoon salt
 1 cup sugar
 ½ cup unsalted butter at room temperature
 1 cup milk
 ½ teaspoon pure vanilla extract
 1 pint fresh raspberries or 1 12-ounce package
   frozen whole unsweetened raspberries
 4 extra large egg whites
   Raspberry Frosting (optional)

GARNISH: fresh or candied violets or rose petals

Preheat the oven to 375°. Butter two muffin tins or line them with paper baking cups. If you have only one muffin tin, line it with baking cups and bake the cupcakes in batches.

Measure ¼ cup of the cake flour and reserve for use with frozen raspberries only. Sift the remaining cake flour again with the baking powder, baking soda, and salt. Cream the sugar and butter together until light and fluffy.

Mix the milk and vanilla. Add the flour mixture to the butter mixture in three batches, alternating with the milk and stirring after each addition until the batter is smooth.

If you are using frozen raspberries, toss with the reserved ¼ cup sifted cake flour. Gently stir the fresh or frozen raspberries into the batter.

Beat the egg whites until stiff but not dry. Stir about one-quarter of the beaten whites into the batter to lighten it. Fold the rest of the whites into the batter in three batches, being careful not to deflate them.

Spoon the batter into the tins, filling the cups half full. Bake for 20 to 25 minutes, until a tester comes out clean. Cool cupcakes in the tins, or if you are baking in batches, remove and cool on racks. When cool, frost with Raspberry Frosting and garnish with the fresh or candied flowers.

RASPBERRY FROSTING

MAKES APPROXIMATELY 1½ CUPS, ENOUGH FOR
24 CUPCAKES OR A 1-LAYER CAKE

¼ cup seedless raspberry jam or jelly
3 tablespoons unsalted butter, softened
3 cups sifted confectioners' sugar
1 tablespoon lemon juice
1 or 2 drops red food coloring (optional)

Heat the jam or jelly in a heavy saucepan over low heat until melted. Measure 3 tablespoons of the melted jam into a bowl. Cool to just warm, about 80°. Cream the butter into the jam. Stir in 1 cup confectioners' sugar. Add the lemon juice. Add the remaining confectioners' sugar gradually. The frosting should be smooth and spreadable; add a little more lemon juice or jam if necessary.

Place wax paper directly on the frosting and let it stand for 15 or 20 minutes before using.

SUMMER
SEAFOOD
DINNER

MENU

Smoked Bluefish Salad

Maryland-Style Baked Fish

Baked Tomatoes with Chive Vinaigrette

Succotash Pudding

Lemon Angel Cake with Blueberries and Cream (page 165)

Maryland White Wine

We chose a beautiful country location in Howard County, Maryland, to present this menu of Chesapeake summer flavors. The stone house on this farm, named By His Grace, dates from 1790 and is situated on 20 acres surrounded by pastureland. We served dinner on the lawn overlooking the pond just behind the house. The Maryland Seyval Blanc we selected was a good complement to both fish courses, but if you cannot find this wine, a Sauvignon Blanc will work as well.

The sunset over the rolling hills, the flickering fireflies and glowing candles, the elegant simplicity of the food and the table created a mood of quiet enjoyment.

SMOKED BLUEFISH SALAD

SERVES 6 TO 8

2 smoked bluefish, about 1¼ pounds each (page 125)
2 heads butter lettuce
⅔ cup sour cream
2 to 4 tablespoons heavy cream
Approximately 4 teaspoons lemon juice
2 tablespoons capers
Salt and freshly ground black pepper
Lemon slices for garnish

Fillet the fish and remove the skin. Flake the fish into large pieces. Clean the lettuce and arrange it on salad plates.

Mix the sour cream, heavy cream, and lemon juice with the capers. Season lightly with salt and pepper.

Arrange the fish on the lettuce and spoon a little dressing over each portion. Garnish the plates with lemon and pass the rest of the dressing.

MARYLAND-STYLE BAKED FISH

SERVES 6 TO 8

1 3- to 4-pound whole fish: white bass, black bass, striped bass, Atlantic red snapper, or Pacific rock cod
7 or 8 medium mushrooms, about ¼ pound
3 tablespoons unsalted butter
Approximately 2 cups day-old breadcrumbs, loosely packed
¼ cup chopped chives
½ teaspoon salt
⅛ teaspoon ground cloves
Few dashes of cayenne pepper
3 or 4 tablespoons heavy cream
1 cup dry white wine
1 cup water
1 lemon, cut into thin slices

GARNISH: **sliced lemon**
chive sprigs

Gut and scale the fish or have the fishmonger do this. Remove the eyes if desired.

Chop the mushrooms very fine and sauté in 1½ tablespoons of the butter for a few minutes. Cool the mushrooms, then mix with the bread crumbs, chives, salt, cloves, and cayenne pepper. Moisten the mixture lightly with 3 or 4 tablespoons of cream. Stuff the cavity of the fish with the mushroom mixture. Sew the fish with cooking twine in a loose overstitch, or skewer the fish closed.

Preheat the oven to 550°. Heat the wine and water to boiling in a small pan. Butter a baking dish or tray large enough to hold the fish.

Place the fish in the buttered dish and pour in the hot wine and water. Dot the top of the fish with the remaining butter and place several lemon slices on top. Bake at 550° for 10 minutes, then reduce heat to 425°. Bake for about 30 minutes, or until the fish is done.*

Remove the thread or skewers. Transfer the fish carefully to a warm serving platter and garnish with lemon and chives. Serve hot.

There are two principal ways to test fish for doneness. The pressure test, similar to that used for meats, calls for pressing the thickest part of the fish with your finger. If the flesh is firm yet springy, the fish is done. This method requires some practice, but is good to learn because no cutting is required. Otherwise, make a small slit with a sharp knife in the thick flesh just behind the gills. If done, the flesh will be opaque and flake easily.

BAKED TOMATOES WITH CHIVE VINAIGRETTE

SERVES 6 TO 8

4 medium firm, ripe tomatoes
4 tablespoons olive oil
4 teaspoons red wine or balsamic vinegar
4 tablespoons fresh chopped chives
   Salt and freshly ground black pepper

Preheat the oven to 400°. Core the tomatoes and cut in half crosswise. Place them on a foil-lined baking sheet and bake about 10 minutes.

While the tomatoes are baking, mix the remaining ingredients. After the tomatoes have cooked 10 minutes, spoon the vinaigrette over them. Bake 5 minutes longer and serve hot.

SUCCOTASH PUDDING

SERVES 6 TO 8

3 tablespoons unsalted butter
1 medium onion, diced
3 ears fresh sweet corn, cut from the cob, about 1½ cups kernels
1½ pounds fresh lima beans, shelled, or 10 ounces frozen baby lima beans
3 extra large eggs
1½ cups half-and-half
3 tablespoons all-purpose flour
   Salt and freshly ground black pepper to taste
1 cup grated Emmenthal or Jarlsberg cheese

Generously butter a round or oval 1½-quart gratin dish. Preheat the oven to 375°.

Melt the butter in a large skillet, add the onion, and soften it for about 15 minutes over medium-low heat. Add the corn and limas and cook for 7 or 8 minutes. Remove the pan from the heat.

Whisk the eggs with the half-and-half. Whisk in the flour. Season well with salt and pepper. Stir the vegetables and ⅔ cup of the cheese into the egg mixture. Pour into the buttered dish. Sprinkle with the remaining cheese.

Bake about 25 minutes, until the top is a rich golden brown. Before serving, let the pudding stand for 5 minutes, then cut into wedges.

—

COCKTAIL
PARTY

—

MENU

Oysters with Fresh Horseradish Sauce

Clams on the Half Shell with Relish or Chili Sauce

French-Fried Sweet Potatoes

Fried Soft Shell Clams

Ham Biscuits with Honey Mustard

Squash and Red Pepper Muffins

Spinach and Blue Cheese Dip

Maryland and Virginia White and Red Wines

The Ladew Topiary Gardens in Monkton, Maryland, provided a charming setting for our cocktail party, which took place on a fine autumn afternoon. The original house, built in 1740, was enlarged in 1850 to become a manor house. Harvey S. Ladew, a wealthy art collector, bought the property in 1929, and continued to make renovations to the house and design its surrounding gardens until his death in 1976. He filled the house with wonderful *objets d'art* and created the finest topiary garden in the United States; the house and gardens now comprise a museum that is open to the public. Among the art collections is an unusual one that reflects Mr. La-

dew's love for the hunt or fox chase: pieces of china, silver, crystal, even furniture and rugs wrought with hunting scenes, foxes, horses, horns, and hounds.

Before the party, our guests strolled in the formal gardens and viewed the famous topiaries, whose shapes range from a fox and hounds to a Buddha. Then everyone gathered in the house to sample the menu, which offered an assortment of appetizers suited to the season. To amplify the mood of autumnal lushness, the manor was filled with an abundance of fancifully arranged garden flowers.

When you plan a cocktail party such as this one, to serve from 12 to 16 people, remember that the yield of the appetizers will increase as the number of varieties increases. For example, Oysters with Fresh Horseradish Sauce serves six to eight as a single appetizer, but will serve two to three times as many people when part of a menu with four to six other appetizers. Maryland and Virginia wines are natural partners to the menu. If they are not available to you, substitute other wines, such as Sauvignon Blanc and Pinot Noir.

OYSTERS WITH FRESH HORSERADISH SAUCE

We have offered two versions of this recipe: one for those who like their oysters on the half shell; the other for those who like cooked oysters.

SERVES 6 TO 8

OYSTERS ON THE HALF SHELL

3 dozen fresh oysters
2 tablespoons freshly grated horseradish, or to taste
2 tablespoons white wine vinegar
2 tablespoons water
1 medium shallot, diced fine

Shuck the oysters (page 21) and arrange them on the half shells on a platter lined with crushed ice. Mix the horseradish, vinegar, water, and shallot in a bowl. Put a small amount of sauce on each oyster, or put the sauce in a pretty little bowl and pass with a small spoon so guests can sauce their own.

BROILED OYSTERS

3 dozen fresh oysters
   Rock salt, about 5 pounds
2 tablespoons freshly grated horseradish, or to taste
3 tablespoons heavy cream
1 tablespoon sour cream
1 medium shallot, diced fine

Preheat the oven to broil. Shuck the oysters. Spread a thick layer of rock salt on a large baking sheet. Put the oysters on the half shells on the rock salt so that they do not tip and lose their juices. Spread more rock salt on one or two large platters.

Combine the horseradish, heavy cream, and sour cream. Stir in the shallot. Put about half a teaspoon of the sauce on each oyster. Broil 6 inches from the flame, until the oysters just begin to curl at the edges, about 5 minutes. Arrange on the serving platter and serve hot.

CLAMS ON THE HALF SHELL WITH RELISH OR CHILI SAUCE

This recipe offers two condiments to bring out the flavor of clams. One uses fresh peppers; the other is a traditional recipe made with Mrs. Besson's Chili Sauce. For this preparation use the smallest size hard shell clams available.

SERVES 6

36 to 48 littleneck clams
   Crushed ice or rock salt for presentation
   Fresh Pepper Relish
   Chili Sauce

Scrub the clams well. Shuck them (page 17), being careful to retain their juices, and pick out any pieces of shell or grit with the point of the clam knife. Do not rinse the clams unless they are very gritty. Arrange them on a platter of crushed ice or rock salt. They may be shucked an hour or so before serving and kept covered in the refrigerator.

To serve, garnish each clam with about ¼ teaspoon of the relish and serve the rest of the relish in a small dish. If using Chili Sauce, serve separately.

FRESH PEPPER RELISH

⅓ cup finely chopped red sweet pepper
⅓ cup finely chopped green sweet pepper
 1 shallot, chopped fine, about 1½ tablespoons
1½ teaspoons finely chopped fresh oregano
1½ teaspoons finely chopped fresh parsley
 1 tablespoon white wine vinegar, or lemon juice
 1 tablespoon olive oil
   Freshly ground black pepper, or a dash of cayenne
   Salt

Mix the peppers, shallot, herbs, vinegar or lemon juice, and olive oil in a small bowl. Season lightly with pepper or cayenne pepper and salt. Cover and place in the refrigerator for a few hours. Let stand at room temperature 15 minutes before serving.

CHILI SAUCE

¾ cup Mrs. Besson's Chili Sauce (page 171)
 1 tablespoon freshly grated or prepared horseradish
   Few drops lemon juice

Mix the chili sauce and horseradish together in a bowl and season with lemon juice. Refrigerate until ready to use. Serve at room temperature.

The cutting gardens at Ladew provided the late-blooming roses and early fall foliage for this unusual swag, above left, on the Manor House front door.

Mr. Ladew gave rein to one of his favorite pursuits, and to his sense of humor, in this realistic topiary of the fox chase, above.

Antique china and fox chase bibelots provide the backdrop for a selection of appetizers, left—French-Fried Sweet Potatoes and Fried Soft Shell Clams with Tartar Sauce, and vegetables with Spinach and Blue Cheese Dip.

Louanne Sargent, one of the guests, right, offers a silver platter of Squash and Red Pepper Muffins.

FRENCH-FRIED SWEET POTATOES

French fries are of passionate interest here. Some shops in beach resorts sell only french fries (made with white potatoes), and vie with one another for the title of best in town. French-fried sweet potatoes can be found at seafood festivals and fairs. Sometimes they are sprinkled with cinnamon sugar rather than seafood seasoning.

SERVES 6

4 large sweet potatoes
  Peanut or vegetable oil
  Chesapeake seafood seasoning

Scrub the potatoes and peel if desired. Cut lengthwise into ⅜-inch strips.

Heat the oil to about 325°. Fry the potatoes in small batches, about 3 minutes for each batch. Drain on paper towels and cool for at least 10 minutes before the final frying. At this stage, the potatoes may be held uncovered at room temperature for 2 or 3 hours.

For the final frying, heat the oil to about 375°. Fry the potatoes in small batches, until golden brown, about 4 minutes for each batch. Drain on paper towels and sprinkle each batch with seafood seasoning. Keep the finished batches in a warm oven while frying the remaining potatoes. Serve immediately.

FRIED SOFT SHELL CLAMS

The delicacy of these fried clams is achieved by using a tempura-style batter instead of the traditional heavier batter, which results in a rather leaden dish with little clam flavor.

SERVES 4 TO 6

3 to 4 dozen soft shell clams
  Abundant oil for frying
2 cups sifted unbleached white flour
2 tablespoons Chesapeake seafood seasoning
2 egg yolks
2 cups ice water

GARNISH: lemon wedges

OPTIONAL SAUCES: Lemon Seafood Sauce (page 173) or Tartar Sauce (page 174), Mrs. Besson's Chili Sauce (page 171) or Fresh Horseradish Sauce (pages 64 and 65)

Scrub the clams well. Shuck them (see page 17), remove from the shells, and discard the necks. Rinse the clams if they are very sandy.

Begin heating the oil in a large deep pan; a wok works well for this recipe. When the oil is just a couple of minutes from being hot, about 390°, make the batter.

Add 1 cup of the flour to a large bowl and stir in 1 tablespoon of seafood seasoning. Whisk 1 egg yolk lightly with 1 cup of ice water. Stir this mixture rapidly into the flour, using the handle of a wooden spoon. Do not overmix; there should be lumps in the batter.

Quickly dip about one-quarter of the clams into the batter to coat them well. Transfer the clams to the oil with a large slotted spoon, separating them with another spoon as you drop them into the oil. The clams will be done when they are a nice golden brown, about 3 minutes when the oil is at the right temperature. Turn them to brown evenly.

Drain the clams on paper towels. Coat another one-quarter of the clams with the batter and fry.

Make another batch of batter with the remaining ingredients and fry the rest of the clams. Be sure that you get to eat some of this batch!

It's best to serve each batch while still hot before frying the next. Garnish the serving platter with lemon wedges, and pass the sauce separately.

HAM BISCUITS WITH HONEY MUSTARD

Country-cured hams require soaking and long cooking before they can be eaten. Follow the maker's direction for this procedure. We find that soaking for an extra day beyond what is specified improves the flavor of most hams. The water should be changed two or three times every twenty-four hours. You can also buy this ham—sliced and ready to eat—by the pound in some delicatessens.

MAKES APPROXIMATELY 30 BISCUITS
SERVES 8 TO 12

1 recipe Ginny Glenn's Angel Biscuits (page 98),
   cut into 1½-inch rounds
1 pound cooked country-cured ham, such as
   Smithfield
   Honey Mustard (page 173)
   Approximately 4 tablespoons unsalted butter,
   softened

Split the biscuits. Slice the cooked and cooled ham into very thin slices; shaved is perhaps a better description of how the ham should be cut.

Spread one side of the biscuits with some honey mustard and the other side with butter. Distribute the slivers of ham between the biscuit halves.

The biscuits may be cut and the ham sliced ahead, but the biscuits are better assembled shortly before serving. To hold assembled biscuits for an hour or so, cover them very well with plastic wrap and foil.

SQUASH AND RED PEPPER MUFFINS

This recipe makes good use of leftover cooked winter squash —butternut, acorn, or pumpkin. The red pepper may be roasted and peeled, or used uncooked; both versions are good. The miniature muffins make a tasty, different party bread.

MAKES 40 MINIATURE MUFFINS, OR
12 REGULAR MUFFINS

1⅓ cups unbleached white flour
  2 teaspoons baking powder
  1 teaspoon salt
 ½ cup milk
  2 extra large eggs, separated
  2 tablespoons vegetable oil or melted butter
 ⅔ cup puréed squash or pumpkin
 ½ cup finely diced sweet red pepper
  1 tablespoon finely diced shallot

Preheat the oven to 350°. Butter and flour the muffin tins. Mix the flour, baking powder, and salt in a large bowl. Mix the milk, egg yolks, and oil in another bowl. In a separate bowl, combine the squash purée, red pepper, and shallot. Beat the egg whites until stiff but not dry.

Stir the milk mixture into the bowl with flour. Stir in the squash mixture rapidly. Stir in half of the beaten egg whites to lighten the mixture, then fold in the rest. Fill the prepared muffin tins about two-thirds full.

Bake miniature muffins for about 20 minutes, and regular muffins about 30 minutes, until a tester comes out clean, changing the position of the tins halfway through the baking. Serve hot or warm.

If you are making the muffins ahead, remove them from the pans about 5 minutes after they come from the oven. Cool on racks, then wrap tightly in foil and store at room temperature. For longer storage, freeze on baking sheets, then wrap for the freezer. The muffins will keep frozen for 2 to 4 weeks. To serve, unwrap and place the frozen muffins on a baking sheet. Heat at 350° for 15 to 20 minutes.

SPINACH AND BLUE CHEESE DIP

Bright color and flavor make this dip appealing. Serve it with sweet red, yellow, and green pepper strips and blanched cauliflower for a festive look and complementary taste.

MAKES 2 CUPS

  6 ounces fresh spinach
  5 ounces blue cheese
 ⅓ cup half-and-half
  1 small garlic clove, peeled
 ¼ teaspoon salt
   Pinch of cayenne
   Freshly ground black pepper

Stem the spinach and wash it well. Drain well, place in a pan, cover tightly, and wilt over low heat in the water that clings to the leaves for a minute or so. Drain well in a colander, pressing but not squeezing, to extract extra liquid.

Transfer the spinach to a food processor. Crumble the blue cheese over it and add the half-and-half. Process for about 30 seconds, dropping the garlic clove in while the machine is running. Stop and scrape down the sides of the processor. Add the salt, cayenne, and black pepper to taste. Process until the mixture is very smooth.

Cover and chill the dip for at least 1 hour before serving. The dip can also be made up to one day ahead, in which case, remove it from the refrigerator for 20 to 30 minutes before serving. Adjust the seasoning as necessary and serve at room temperature.

—

HUNT
BREAKFAST

—

MENU

Chesapeake Nuts

Old-Style Clam Chowder

Joyce's Vinegared Ham

Sweet Potato Rolls (page 56)

**Bread and Butter Pickles with
Horseradish**

Celeriac and Turkey Salad

Tangy Waldorf Salad

Rosy Applesauce

Black Walnut Cookies

Gingerbread

**Chesapeake Hard and Soft
Cider**

The fox chase, though a sport involving a small number of participants, is well represented in many locales around the Chesapeake. At the Howard County Hunt Club in Maryland, where our hunt breakfast took place, riders were out early to take the stirrup cup, a ritual small glass of sherry. Then riders and hounds were off over the hilly wooded country, following the intricate, centuries' old traditions of the fox chase.

Johnny Bill Lenton, the huntsman, keeps on close terms with the eager and affectionate hounds. He knows over sixty by name and recognizes which ones to call to order in a field pack of thirty to forty. All hounds do not go out on a given hunt and some who stayed behind showed a strong interest in the breakfast we had prepared for the riders.

Breakfast, as with many terms of the hunt, is actually something else, in this case, lunch or brunch. It takes place after the chase, and depending on the importance of the hunt, may be an elaborate catered affair or an alfresco picnic. Our breakfast was informal since it followed a cubbing—a training chase for young hounds. For this event, riders do not wear their pinks (in fact, red coats), but their greens. At formal hunt breakfasts, rather substantial food is served: ham, roast quail, goose or beef, soups, salads, a variety of beverages, and a choice of desserts. For our menu, we kept the tradition of a hearty meal for hungry riders.

CHESAPEAKE NUTS

MAKES APPROXIMATELY 3½ CUPS

1 pound raw shelled and skinned peanuts, or a
   mixture of peanuts and raw shelled pecans
1½ tablespoons vegetable oil
1 tablespoon Old Bay or other Chesapeake
   seafood seasoning

Preheat oven to 350°. Toss the nuts in the vegetable
oil. Spread the nuts on an ungreased baking pan and
toast them for about 10 minutes. When they begin to
color, remove them from oven and toss with the seafood seasoning. Toast 2 to 4 minutes longer, until
they are aromatic and golden brown. Cool to room
temperature and serve, or store the nuts in a tightly
closed container.

OLD-STYLE CLAM CHOWDER

*This is a very flavorful clam chowder that uses neither
tomatoes nor cream and flour. It is our variation of a recipe
from* Fifty Years in a Maryland Kitchen *by Mrs. B. C.
Howard.*

SERVES 4 TO 6

1½ to 2 dozen chowder clams
  2 tablespoons olive or vegetable oil
  1 celery rib, diced fine
½ medium onion, diced fine
  2 to 3 cups veal broth
  1 large sprig savory or thyme, or ¼ teaspoon
    dried savory or thyme leaves
  2 medium potatoes, peeled and diced
  2 medium carrots, peeled and diced
½ cup corn kernels and/or ½ cup shelled fresh
    peas (optional)
    Salt and freshly ground black pepper

Scrub the clams well and place in a pan large enough
to hold them in one layer. Add 1 cup of water. Cover
the pan with a tight-fitting lid and steam the clams
open. When they are cool enough to handle, remove
the clams from the shells, discarding the tough muscles.

Strain the clam broth through tightly woven
cheesecloth or paper towels. If the clams are very

gritty, rinse them in the broth and strain the broth
again. Chop the clams coarsely.

Meanwhile, soften the celery and onion in the oil
in a soup pot over low heat. Add the clam broth, veal
broth, and herbs to the softened vegetables. Add the
potatoes and carrots. Cook the soup for about 10 minutes.

Add the chopped clams and cook for 10 minutes
longer, adding the corn and/or peas during the last 5
minutes of cooking. Taste for seasoning and serve
hot.

JOYCE'S VINEGARED HAM

*A humble picnic ham is quite transformed by this prepara-
tion. Our friend Joyce DeBaggio takes it along for a week-
end at her family home on the Potomac. It's best for
sandwiches, but it is also tasty served warm with mashed
potatoes and cooked greens.*

SERVES 6 TO 10

  1 8- to 10-pound picnic or regular bone-in ham
  5 or 6 large garlic cloves
12 cups water
  2 cups apple cider vinegar
  4 or 5 sprigs oregano, about 6 inches long, or
    1½ teaspoons dried oregano leaves
  2 or 3 small dried whole chiles, such as cayenne
    peppers

Trim the ham of rind and exterior fat. Peel the garlic
and cut it into slivers. Cut evenly spaced slits all over
the ham with a boning knife or a thin, narrow knife
and insert the garlic slivers.

Choose a noncorrodible pot large enough to hold
the ham when the lid is on. Add the water and vinegar—the liquid should come about halfway up the
ham. Add a little more water if necessary. Add the
oregano and chiles.

Bring the liquid to a simmer and cook the ham
for 20 minutes per pound. Turn occasionally and
keep the liquid just at a simmer. If you are cooking
the ham ahead for slicing later, cool it in the liquid
and store it in the refrigerator in the covered pot.

For sandwiches, slice the ham thin. To serve hot,
slice it ¼ inch thick.

A long fall morning's chase whets appetites for this hearty breakfast, left, of Old-Style Clam Chowder, Vinegared Ham Sandwiches, Bread and Butter Pickles, and Tangy Waldorf Salad.

The chase begins early, with the stirrup cup, below—a small glass of sherry—to fortify the riders until they can breakfast.

The first English fox hounds were brought to Maryland during the colonial period. Johnny Bill Lenton, Master of the Hounds, right, keeps his charges at heel.

HUNT BREAKFAST

BREAD AND BUTTER PICKLES WITH HORSERADISH

────

The recipe may be doubled if you have cucumbers waiting on the vine. The small, rough-skinned pickling cucumbers make the best pickles. Of the many varieties, perhaps gherkin and kirby are most common.

MAKES 3 PINTS

1½ pounds pickling cucumbers
 2 medium onions
 3 tablespoons salt
 1 cup water
 4 cups ice cubes
1½ cups sugar
 2 cups distilled vinegar
 1 tablespoon mustard seed
 6 whole cloves
 1 teaspoon dill seed
 ½ teaspoon celery seed
 1 1-ounce piece fresh horseradish root

Scrub the cucumbers well. Peel the onions. Slice the vegetables about ⅛ inch thick. Toss in a large bowl with the salt, water, and ice cubes. Cover the bowl with a plate and weight with a heavy pan or canned goods. Let stand at room temperature for 4 hours.

Drain the vegetables, cover tightly, and refrigerate overnight.

Mix the sugar, vinegar, mustard, cloves, dill, and celery seed together in a bowl. Stir to dissolve the sugar a bit.

Sterilize canning jars, rings, and lids according to the manufacturer's directions.

Peel the horseradish root and cut into julienne. Add the horseradish, cucumbers, and onions to a large, noncorrodible pan. Pour the pickling liquid over the mixture and bring to a simmer. The bubbles should just break the surface; do not overcook. Remove from the heat as soon as the mixture begins to simmer.

Immediately pack the pickles in the hot, sterilized jars. Pour the liquid over the pickles, leaving ½-inch head space. Seal the jars, according to the manufacturer's directions, and process in a boiling water bath for 10 minutes. Remove the jars, cover with a towel, and let cool to room temperature. Check the seals; store any unsealed jars in the refrigerator and use them as soon as possible. Wait at least a week before using the sealed pickles.

CELERIAC AND TURKEY SALAD

────

Fresh tarragon, or tarragon preserved in vinegar, is a good addition here, but the dried herb will add an acrid, musty flavor. This salad will keep well if you want to make it a day ahead.

SERVES 4 TO 6

 2 pounds celeriac
 1 lemon
   Approximately ½ pound cooked turkey
 ⅓ cup plain yogurt
 ⅓ cup sour cream
 2 tablespoons Dijon-style mustard
 ⅓ cup mayonnaise
 1 tablespoon capers
 ¼ cup snipped chives or scallions, sliced thin
 2 tablespoons parsley, chopped
   Salt and freshly ground black pepper
 2 or 3 fresh tarragon sprigs, stemmed and leaves chopped (optional)

Peel the celeriac knobs and rub well with a cut lemon. Squeeze the lemon into a bowl with cold water. Julienne the celeriac and drop the pieces into the bowl.

Julienne the turkey. Mix the yogurt, sour cream, mustard, and mayonnaise together with the capers, chives, parsley, and tarragon, if using.

Drain the celeriac pieces and pat dry. Toss with the turkey and dressing. Season the salad with salt and pepper, and more mustard, if desired. Marinate, covered, in the refrigerator for 2 hours or longer. Let the salad cool to room temperature before serving.

═══════════

TANGY WALDORF SALAD

────

SERVES 4 TO 6

 1 large celery rib
 2 medium tart, crisp apples
 ½ cup walnut pieces
 ⅓ cup currants or raisins
 ¼ cup mayonnaise
 ¼ cup yogurt
2½ tablespoons freshly grated horseradish

Slice the celery crosswise into ¼-inch slices. Wash and core the apples. Cut them lengthwise into thin slices. Toss the celery, apples, walnuts, and currants or raisins in a bowl.

Add the mayonnaise, yogurt, and horseradish and blend well. The salad is best if it stands for at least 30 minutes before serving. Serve at cool room temperature.

ROSY APPLESAUCE

This sauce has a pretty pink tint because the skins are left on during the cooking, then sieved through a food mill. The recipe is for a small quantity, but it can easily be doubled or tripled.

MAKES ABOUT 2 CUPS

6 large apples, Stayman or Winesap
1 to 2 tablespoons lemon juice
⅓ cup sugar (optional)
    Pinch ground cinnamon and nutmeg (optional)

Core the apples and roughly chop. Place in a heavy saucepan and stir in the lemon juice and sugar, if using. Cover and cook over low heat for 30 to 40 minutes, stirring occasionally so that the apples do not stick and until they have completely softened.

Puree the apples through a food mill. Add cinnamon and nutmeg, if you want extra flavor. Serve warm, or cool to room temperature and store in the refrigerator or freezer until ready to use.

BLACK WALNUT COOKIES

MAKES 6 DOZEN COOKIES

1 cup sugar
1 extra large egg
1 cup unsalted butter, cut into 16 pieces
1 teaspoon pure vanilla extract
2 cups unbleached white flour
½ teaspoon salt
4 ounces black walnuts, finely ground

In a food processor, combine the sugar with the egg and process for 1 minute. Add the butter and vanilla and process for another minute.

Mix the flour and salt together and add to the processor. Process 20 seconds, until the flour is almost incorporated. Add the walnuts and pulse just until mixed; do not overprocess.

Using plastic wrap, roll the dough into three cylinders, 1½ to 2 inches wide. Chill for about an hour, until the dough is firm, or freeze for 15 minutes.

Preheat the oven to 350°. Slice the dough slightly less than ¼ inch thick with a sharp knife. Place the rounds ½ inch apart on baking sheets. Bake until the edges are golden brown, 10 to 12 minutes. Remove the cookies from the baking sheets immediately and cool on racks. Store in tightly covered tins.

GINGERBREAD

MAKES 1 8-INCH-SQUARE BREAD

1⅔ cups unbleached white flour
1 teaspoon baking powder
½ teaspoon salt
2½ teaspoons powdered ginger
¼ teaspoon ground mace
¼ teaspoon ground cloves
⅛ teaspoon mustard powder
6 tablespoons unsalted butter, softened
⅓ cup dark brown sugar
2 extra large eggs
½ cup unsulfured molasses
⅔ cup hot water
1 teaspoon baking soda

Preheat the oven to 350°. Butter an 8-inch-square baking pan.

Sift the dry ingredients together, except for the baking soda. Cream the butter and sugar in a mixer and add the eggs, mixing well.

Mix the molasses and hot water and stir into the soda. Add the flour mixture to the creamed butter in three batches, alternately with the molasses mixture.

Pour the batter into the prepared baking pan and bake for about 25 minutes, until a cake tester comes out clean.

CHESAPEAKE
RECIPES

The genius of Chesapeake cooking resides in the home. It was in family kitchens rather than in restaurants that the great majority of dishes were first created. Being invited to dinner by a good cook still affords one the best opportunity of tasting the finest Chesapeake food. But home-based cooking is one of the most important distinguishing marks of any great regional cuisine. Whether the local ingredients are abundant, as is the case in the Chesapeake, or few, talent, ingenuity, and sheer love of cooking must characterize a large number of cooks in all social classes. In our recipe introductions we outline some of the conditions that foster this region's culinary development.

It is a particular pleasure to bring Chesapeake cuisine to the public's notice because the recipes are accessible to anyone interested in cooking good food without having to use exotic ingredients and time-consuming techniques. During our research for this book of both historical and contemporary sources, we were much impressed with the results Chesapeake cooks have achieved with three common-sense tenets: respect for local ingredients; close observation of the matter at hand, whether it be bread or goose; and a regard for the taste of things themselves.

Our task of selecting recipes was daunting only in that there were so many excellent ones to choose from. For example, we considered a dozen versions of the justifiably famous Crab Imperial. The not unpleasant work of preparing and tasting several resulted in the two recipes we've included—Crab Imperials in their best Chesapeake form.

The important respect in which we have altered traditional dishes is by reducing the use of fats. In the Chesapeake region, as in the rest of the United States, the modern way of life requires fewer calories, and the importance of a healthful diet is better understood than even a decade ago. While some recipes are lighter, and we think tastier, than the original versions, the main ingredients and flavorings are in place to give a true taste of the Chesapeake.

APPETIZERS AND FIRST COURSES

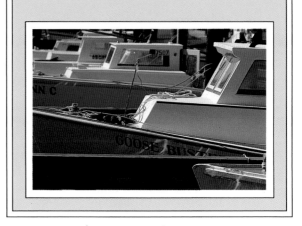

The ideal appetizer is one that is light, simple, fresh, pleasing to the eye, with a distinctive but not overpowering flavor. Oysters and clams on the half shell almost perfectly fit the description. Fresh from local water, they gleam handsomely in their own serving containers, and their tingling sweet-salt sea taste and satisfying lightness stimulate the appetite for the meal to follow. When Chesapeake cooks think of first courses, they naturally turn to the Bay with its abundance of bivalves.

The custom of beginning a meal with something small and light has evolved slowly here. In colonial times dinners did not include appetizers as we know them; diners plunged *in medias res*. In the poorer households only the basics—bread and soup—were served. For the well-to-do, however, a typical meal included a "first course" of eight or ten dishes, followed by a "second course" of six or eight dishes plus tarts, custards, cakes, or jellies, and finished with fruits and nuts. Each "course" was a complete meal in itself: soups; roasted, baked, and broiled meats; fish and fowl, with and without sauces; and vegetables. To us, this may seem more like Thanksgiving dinner, and in an important way it was. Abundance was a blessing to be shared. But by the time *Fifty Years in a Maryland Kitchen*, a justifiably famous cookbook by Mrs. B. C. Howard, was published in 1873, this style of lavish dining was no longer fashionable, even among the well-to-do. Mrs. Howard's book does not include appetizers because meals in her time customarily commenced with soup.

During the later nineteenth century, it was the expanding middle class that established the patterns of consumption, and the niceties of what to serve when, for people of all classes. Eating styles began to change again in the twentieth century when fewer people were engaged in strenuous physical labor, the pace of life quickened, and more restaurants began to open. Today, concerns with health and diet practically mandate moderate beginnings; nevertheless, there's no fetish of light eating around the Chesapeake. Appetizers here are meant to stimulate the appetite.

With occasional exceptions for elegant dinners, the Chesapeake takes an informal approach to appetizers. Of course, oysters and clams on the half shell fit wonderfully into any menu, whether for a backyard barbecue or the most formal reception. But the raw bar, popular as it is, is not the only prelude, nor is preparation limited to the understatement of the shucker's skill. Clams and oysters are stuffed, baked, or broiled and served with various sauces. Deep-fried tidbits are also very popular, especially soft shell clams or oysters in batter, or crab shaped into small cakes. Smoked fish, crab-stuffed tomatoes, or crab with melon make small first course salads, and crab finds its way into little pastry cases or tartlets, or into the chafing dish as crab dip or fondue.

Although the waters of the Chesapeake are the main source for appetizers, other areas of the region supply variety enough to satisfy those who don't care for seafood. Vegetables and bread-based nibbles make occasional but important appearances. Mushrooms stuffed with seafood, cheese, or herbs are well liked, and recently raw vegetables have found a place on the menu. Curiously, appetizers rarely are made from pork, an important ingredient—especially cured pork—in Chesapeake cuisine. The exception is Ham Biscuits, which are traditional and very good. They usually are made with country-cured ham, an import from inland Virginia that has found a home around the Chesapeake. Since they are considered a regional delicacy, Ham Biscuits are frequently served at dinners designed to impress, or at elegant affairs. We think they're fine picnic food, too, when they're put together on the spot.

The main venues for appetizers in the Chesapeake region are parties and restaurants, with the focus on simple, popular dishes. There are uncommonly few timbales or pâtés to be found here. Borrowing from other cuisines does occur, but usually only simple recipes, which are adapted to local ingredients. The home cook does not include appetizers on the daily menu, but soups, especially seafood soups, are still favored first courses. The idea of something to perk up the appetite, or temporarily assuage it, has slowly found currency in home-cooking. Spicy-good deviled eggs may start a Sunday supper, or an elegant dinner may commence with a first course of shad roe. Whatever the occasion, from parties to family gatherings, there are ample choices for delicious beginnings.

DEVILED CLAMS

SERVES 6 TO 8

3 dozen littleneck or cherrystone clams
  Cornmeal
2 ounces (2 slices) thick-sliced bacon
2 scallions, sliced thin with some of the green parts
2 tablespoons Dijon-style mustard
  Dash or two of Tabasco
  Dash of Angostura bitters
  About 4 cups rock salt for lining the baking sheet

Scrub the clams well and soak in cold water with a handful of cornmeal for about 30 minutes. Cut the bacon into ¼-inch dice and cook over low heat until crisp; drain and reserve.

Shuck the clams and place them on a baking sheet lined with rock salt. The clams may be prepared to this point and kept refrigerated an hour or so before broiling.

Mix together the cooked bacon, mustard, and scallions. Season with Tabasco and bitters. Spoon about ¼ teaspoon topping on each clam.

Place the clams in a preheated broiler about 5 inches from the heat and broil until bubbling hot, about 3 minutes. Serve on the baking tray, or on a platter lined with rock salt.

ED CUTTS'S FRIED OYSTERS

Ed Cutts, from Oxford, Maryland, makes these as cleanly as he designs and builds beautiful wooden sailing boats: no pancake mix, no elaborate egg and cracker crumb batter, just the pure taste of succulent golden brown oysters. Ed likes the oysters plain and piping hot, but he serves them with Heinz ketchup mixed with a little horseradish. We like them plain, too, or with Mrs. Besson's Chili Sauce (page 171) and some freshly grated horseradish.

A traditional Eastern Shore church supper dish, chicken salad and fried oysters is another delicious way to serve these. The Chicken and Cucumber Salad (page 156) complements the oysters very well. Yet another tasty use of fried oysters is in oyster loaves. To make these, warm 6 hollowed-out Kaiser rolls before you begin frying the oysters. Some brush the rolls with melted butter, heap them with fried oysters, and serve the loaves with ketchup, horseradish, and lettuce. Others prefer to make a bed of shredded lettuce inside the rolls, then spoon in some tartar sauce and add the fried oysters.

In any kind of deep frying, the more oil the better. For this quantity of oysters, 2 quarts is the minimum amount. Peanut oil has the most dependable smoking point, though other vegetable oils may be used. If you care to strain the cooled used oil through cloth (pieces of old sheets or pillowcases are good for this), you can use it once more for frying seafood. Keep the oil refrigerated until you need it.

SERVES 4 TO 6

4 dozen oysters, freshly shucked, or 2 pints standard oysters
2 quarts peanut oil
3 cups all-purpose flour
2 tablespoons Old Bay® seasoning, or to taste

Drain the freshly shucked oysters, or rinse the packed oysters briefly and drain them. Heat the oil.

Mix the flour with the Old Bay. Dredge the oysters in the flour, a dozen at a time. (Ed shakes them together in a paper bag.) When the oil is at 400°, begin frying the oysters. If you don't have a thermometer, drop a piece of white bread in the oil. If it turns golden brown in 30 to 40 seconds, the oil is ready.

Quickly add the oysters to the hot oil, one at a time, being careful to slide them in so no oil splatters. The oysters will be done and golden brown in 1½ to 2 minutes. Drain on paper towels and serve hot.

CRAB IN CHERRY TOMATOES

SERVES 10 TO 15, ABOUT 65 TOMATOES

  1 pound lump crabmeat
  ½ cup Homemade Mayonnaise (page 174)
  ¼ cup chopped chives
      Few drops lemon juice
      Few drops Tabasco
      Salt to taste
  2 or 3 pints cherry tomatoes, depending on size

Remove the cartilage from the crabmeat. Mix the crab gently with the mayonnaise and chives. Season with lemon juice, Tabasco, and salt.

Wash the tomatoes, cut about one-third from the stem ends, and remove the centers. Fill the tomatoes with the crab salad. Keep refrigerated until 15 minutes before serving.

Skiffs are used for both commercial and sport fishing.

PICKLED OYSTERS

These were a staple during the last half of the nineteenth century when oysters were plentiful and inexpensive. We have seen old recipes that call for a gallon of shucked oysters. They're still an unusual treat for oyster lovers. This recipe may be doubled. The oysters will keep for a month in the refrigerator. We never have any left from this small batch.

SERVES 4 TO 6

  3 dozen oysters, freshly shucked, or 2 pints standard oysters
  2 whole mace blades, or ¼ teaspoon broken mace blades
  2 allspice berries
  1 teaspoon black peppercorns
  ½ cup dry white wine
  ¼ cup white wine vinegar or distilled vinegar
  ¼ teaspoon salt

If you are using freshly shucked oysters, clean them well and reserve all the liquor. Reserve the shells for presentation. Strain the liquor into a noncorrodible saucepan. If you are using bottled oysters, strain the liquor into a saucepan and rinse the oysters briefly in cold water.

Add the mace, allspice, peppercorns, and white wine to the pan of oyster liquor. Bring the mixture to a simmer and cook 10 minutes, skimming occasionally.

Add the oysters and cook for about 3 minutes, until the edges just curl. Skim the liquid if necessary. When the oysters are just done, remove the pan from the heat and add the vinegar and salt. Let the oysters cool to room temperature, then refrigerate. Serve the oysters very cold, on oyster shells if you have them.

Workboats, sailboats, and charter vessels all find dockage at St. Michaels' harbor.

HOT CRAB DIP

This is an adaptation of the recipe former Governor Hughes of Maryland wrote for the Hunt to Harbor *cookbook. It is the tastiest of the many crab dips we have tried. It is usually served with crisp crackers, but we like it with plain toasted croutons made from baguettes.*

SERVES 6 TO 8

  2 shallots, minced
3½ tablespoons unsalted butter
  1 pound backfin or special crabmeat
1½ tablespoons all-purpose flour
  ¾ cup milk
    Salt and freshly ground white pepper to taste
  1 teaspoon lemon juice, or to taste
    Dash of Worcestershire sauce
  ½ cup heavy cream
  ½ tablespoon sherry
  ½ tablespoon cognac

Soften the shallots in 2 tablespoons of the butter over moderate heat. Meanwhile, remove any cartilage from the crabmeat. Set the shallots and the crabmeat aside.

Melt the remaining 1½ tablespoons of butter in a saucepan over low heat. Add the flour and cook the roux for about 5 minutes, being careful that it does not brown. Add the milk and stir the sauce well. Cook it over low heat for 10 minutes or so, stirring occasionally.

Stir the shallots and crabmeat into the sauce. Season the mixture with salt and pepper, lemon juice, and Worcestershire sauce. Stir in the heavy cream. The dip may be made ahead to this point. If you are making it an hour or more before serving, cover and refrigerate.

About 10 minutes before serving, add the sherry and cognac and heat the dip until it is very hot but not simmering. Serve in a chafing dish.

ASPARAGUS WITH HAM AND MUSTARD

SERVES 6 TO 8

24 asparagus spears, about ½ inch in diameter (1¼ to 1½ pounds asparagus)
⅓ pound thinly sliced Smithfield ham (substitute prosciutto if Smithfield ham is not available— the ham should not be paper thin)
¼ cup Homemade Mayonnaise (page 174), or prepared mayonnaise
2 tablespoons Honey Mustard (page 173), or prepared mustard of your choice

Trim the asparagus to about 6 inches long. The remaining stems can be saved to make soup or sauce, if desired. With a sharp paring knife or a vegetable peeler, peel about 1½ inches from the ends of the stalks.

Pan-steam the asparagus in a little water until it is just crisp-tender, 2 or 3 minutes. Refresh the asparagus under cold water and pat dry.

Trim the ham into pieces about 3 inches square. Mix the mayonnaise and mustard together.

Spread a little of the mustard-mayonnaise on the ham and wrap a ham slice around the middle of each asparagus spear. This dish is best assembled just before serving, though the ingredients may be prepared ahead of time.

DEVILED EGGS WITH SEAFOOD SEASONING

SERVES 6 TO 12

6 extra large eggs, hard-cooked
2 tablespoons minced onion
3 tablespoons Homemade Mayonnaise (page 174)
1 tablespoon Dijon-style mustard
1 tablespoon chopped parsley
1 teaspoon Chesapeake seafood seasoning, or to taste
Dash of Angostura bitters
Salt and freshly ground pepper

Halve the eggs crosswise and cut a tiny slice off the pointed end of each half to allow the eggs to stand.

Remove the yolks and sieve or mash them in a bowl. Add the onion, mayonnaise, mustard, parsley, seafood seasoning, bitters, and salt and pepper. Blend the mixture well and taste for seasoning. Add more seafood seasoning or salt and pepper if necessary.

Mound or pipe the yolk mixture into the egg-white halves. Refrigerate and then serve at room temperature. Garnish with a dash of seafood seasoning if desired.

INDIVIDUAL SEAFOOD PIZZAS

MAKES 20 PIZZAS, ABOUT 3 INCHES IN DIAMETER
SERVES 6 TO 10

PIZZA DOUGH

2 teaspoons active dry yeast
¼ cup very warm water
1¼ cups warm water
3½ cups unbleached white flour
½ cup whole wheat flour
2 tablespoons olive oil
1 teaspoon salt

PIZZA TOPPING

5 dozen littleneck clams unshucked
20 shrimp, about ¾ pound
3 garlic cloves
1¼ pounds fresh plum tomatoes
About ½ cup olive oil
Mixed fresh herbs: 3 or 4 parsley sprigs; 2 or 3 basil sprigs; 2 or 3 marjoram or oregano sprigs
Salt and pepper

GARNISH: 10 imported black olives, such as Kalamata
small fresh herb leaves or flowers

Make the pizza dough the night before, or early on the day you plan to serve the pizzas.

Stir the yeast in ¼ cup of very warm water. Let it stand for about 10 minutes, or until foamy, then add it to the rest of the water.

Mix the flours in a bowl and make a well. Gradually stir the water and yeast mixture into the well. Add the olive oil and salt and stir until combined. Gather the dough into a ball and place on a floured surface. Knead for 7 or 8 minutes, until smooth and springy.

Place the dough in a lightly oiled bowl. Cover it and let rise until double in bulk. It is ideal to do this first rise in the refrigerator overnight.

Punch down the dough. Divide it in half, then divide each half into 10 portions. Gently roll the portions into balls on a lightly floured surface and cover with a dampened and well-wrung tea towel.

Let the dough rise until doubled in bulk. This can take from 20 minutes to 1½ hours, depending on whether the dough has been refrigerated.

Preheat the oven to the highest setting, with a baking stone on the lowest shelf 30 minutes before baking the pizzas. If you do not have a baking stone, preheat the oven for 15 minutes at 450°.

Prepare the pizza topping ingredients. Scrub the clams and place them, along with 1 cup of water, in a large pan with a tight-fitting lid. Steam the clams open. When they have opened, remove them to cool.

Poach the shrimp in the clam broth until they just turn pink and are tender, about 2 minutes. Remove the shrimp from the broth.

Remove the clams from their shells and shell and devein the shrimp. If you wish to do this ahead of time, strain the broth through finely woven cheesecloth and store the shelled clams in it. Cover the shelled and deveined shrimp with a dampened towel.

Slice the tomatoes ¼ inch thick. Mince the garlic and mix it with a little of the olive oil. Remove the leaves from the herbs and chop them. Halve and pit the olives.

To assemble the pizzas, shape the dough into rounds, about ¼ inch thick, with the edges slightly thicker. Cover the dough and let it rest and rise in a warm place for about 15 minutes before topping and baking the pizzas.

Prepare the pizzas on a lightly floured baker's paddle, a few at a time, if you are using a baking stone. Or place the dough on a lightly oiled heavy baking sheet and assemble the toppings.

Brush each round of dough lightly with olive oil. Spread with a little minced garlic and sprinkle some chopped herbs on top. Add 3 slices of tomato. Salt and pepper lightly. Arrange 3 clams and 1 shrimp on top and brush them lightly with olive oil.

Bake the pizzas until the crusts are crisp and puffed, about 5 or 6 minutes on a baking stone, or about 10 minutes on a baking sheet.

Take the pizzas from the oven and brush the rims lightly with olive oil again. Garnish with the olive halves and fresh herbs if desired. Serve hot.

STEAMED SHAD ROE AND ASPARAGUS

This is an appetizer course suitable for a fine dinner; the recipe may be easily doubled. It has the essential flavors of April and early May in the Chesapeake region.

SERVES 4

2 pairs shad roe, totaling about ¾ pound
1½ pounds asparagus
4 slices good-quality white bread
1 shallot, cut into fine dice
⅓ cup plus 1 tablespoon dry white wine or champagne
4 tablespoons cold unsalted butter, cut into bits
2 tablespoons heavy cream
Salt and freshly ground white pepper

To separate the roe, carefully cut the center membrane. Rinse the roe, then prick them all over with a fine needle.

Trim and peel the asparagus stalks. Cut the crusts from the bread and toast it. Cut the toast into triangles.

Pan-steam the asparagus in a little water until crisp-tender. Remove the asparagus to a plate and keep just warm.

Steam the roe over simmering water for 6 minutes, turning it carefully halfway through the cooking time.

Meanwhile make the sauce. Simmer the shallot in ⅓ cup of the wine in a small saucepan over medium-high heat until the wine is reduced to about 1 tablespoon. Strain the mixture by pressing it through a fine sieve. Return the liquid to the saucepan and swirl in the remaining tablespoon of wine over high heat for about 10 seconds. Reduce the heat to low and whisk in the butter, a few bits at a time. Add the cream and season the sauce.

Arrange the roe and asparagus on warm plates and nap them with the sauce. Garnish with the toast and serve immediately.

BREADS

The fragrance of warm muffins and the clatter of the muffin tin against the oven door can stir the soul from slumber like no alarm clock can. Marguerite Ridgely Sargent, Susan Belsinger's elegant mother-in-law, awoke to rustling in the kitchen and the aroma of freshly made muffins or biscuits every day when she was growing up in rural Maryland. Her mother liked to be up early, to work in the cool during the summer months, to bring the kitchen to warmth and life in winter to set the tone of the day. Mrs. Ridgely knew precisely how to play her wood stove—furnished from the gently rolling hills surrounding the family home—firing the cool spots evenly and moderating the hot ones.

She was a baker of talent and enthusiasm, admired for her yeast breads and cakes as well as the shortbreads she made daily. Recipes, though important to her, were not as crucial as the quality of the ingredients. Flour was brought fresh from a local mill in 50-pound sacks. Butter and lard had to be the best. Eggs were from her own chickens.

All preparations were done on a wooden kitchen table, which had a metal extension for kneading and rolling dough, except for the beaten biscuits. After Mrs. Ridgely mixed the biscuit dough, her husband would take it to their smokehouse, place it on the wood chopping block, and beat it with the blunt side of a hatchet for at least 30 minutes, until it blistered. Then Mrs. Ridgely would shape and mark the dough and bake the biscuits in a hot oven until they were the palest gold. These biscuits were the mark of a cook who cared.

Our efforts to modernize the preparation of beaten biscuits cannot be counted as an advancement. We have tried working the dough in a food processor, and in a heavy mixer with a dough hook, and we have beaten it with a heavy rolling pin and with a cleaver; none of these methods produced the flaky texture of the old-fashioned beaten biscuit. The dough must be beaten the traditional way with a heavy hatchet or mallet by someone with the strength to deliver resounding blows and the time to finish the job.

Until about 50 years ago, baking was a necessity as well as a tradition for the large number of families who lived, as the Ridgelys did, in rural Maryland. Before convenience stores, it was a matter of fact that flour had to be converted to the daily bread. It was a rewarding chore that was done willingly and, from all accounts, with pride. The women did virtually all the baking; the men toted the flour and beat the biscuits. Marguerite Sargent remembers learning her measures by bagging the flour and sugar in 2-, 5-, and 10-pound sacks.

The Chesapeake's continuing theme of excellence distinguishes the region from many other areas of the United States where home-baking was a necessity. This can be attributed, we think, to several key factors: the relative closeness of homes and consequent sociability; a long agricultural history; the relative ease of obtaining fine-quality ingredients; and an openness to exchanges with newcomers who brought different traditions and tastes.

Fredericksburg, Hagerstown, and Gaithersburg in western Maryland were named for the German settlers welcomed after the Revolutionary War. They came for the land, bringing with them the goals and skills of steady, sober farm families. In this region drained by the Potomac they found fertile soil, sufficient rainfall, and streams enough to power their mills, all requisite for prosperity. They tilled their land, raised crops and cattle on it, and made it the breadbasket of the Chesapeake. Generation after generation, they treated their harvests well in their kitchens and bakeries, producing wholesome loaves of brown bread and white bread, and adding pumpernickel, stollen, and Kaiser rolls from their homeland. These provided a welcome yeasty change from the quick breads that were the staples of the early English settlers.

By the end of the nineteenth century, Jewish immigrants from Eastern Europe had introduced their Sabbath challah and different versions of breads made with the hardy, inexpensive rye. The wealth of bread recipes from settlements all around the Chesapeake was a clear index of the central role bread-making played in the region.

Waffles and pancakes were made with wheat, corn, rice, or buckwheat. Berries, buttermilk, or corn kernels were added to muffin batter. Cracklings were folded into corn pone or spoon breads, which were lightened with beaten eggs. Ingenious cooks made much use of the protean corn, varying their recipes with white and yellow cornmeal, grits, or hominy. Thin batters with little or no leavening were baked at the hearth on iron utensils or boards. There were so many varieties of breakfast breads—baked or griddle-cooked and served with local honey, maple syrup, or molasses—one could easily go a month without eating the same one. (Now it takes most families a year to complete their repertoire of recipes.)

Loaf breads were not as prevalent, but yeast-raised dinner rolls were deemed necessary for feasts and gatherings. And biscuit-making was considered an art. Thin biscuits (what we would call crackers or wafers), yeast biscuits, herbed quick biscuits—all had their place just slightly below beaten biscuits. A fondness for sweets was evidenced in yeasted cinnamon rolls and sticky buns, baking-powder-leavened pumpkin bread, and sweet potato bread. This great diversity in bread is affirmation that Chesapeake cooks have made a toothsome virtue of necessity.

BUTTERMILK CORN BREAD

MAKES ONE 8-INCH-SQUARE CORN BREAD
SERVES 6

1½ cups yellow cornmeal
  1 cup unbleached white flour
  ½ teaspoon baking powder
    Scant teaspoon salt
  1 teaspoon baking soda
1¾ cups buttermilk
  2 tablespoons molasses
  5 tablespoons vegetable oil

Preheat the oven to 350°. Butter an 8-inch-square pan and dust it with about 1 teaspoon of cornmeal.

Mix the dry ingredients together in a bowl. Add the buttermilk and stir well. Add the molasses and oil and stir well.

Pour the batter into the pan. Bake for 35 minutes or until a tester comes out clean. Cool slightly before cutting and serve warm or at room temperature.

HUSH PUPPIES

MAKES APPROXIMATELY 24
SERVES 6 TO 8

  2 cups stone-ground cornmeal
  1 tablespoon all-purpose flour
  1 teaspoon baking soda
  1 teaspoon baking powder
  ¾ teaspoon salt
    Vegetable or peanut oil for deep-frying
1½ cups buttermilk
  1 bunch scallions, trimmed to 6 inches and chopped fine
  1 extra large egg

Combine the cornmeal, flour, baking soda, baking powder, and salt in a large bowl. Heat the oil to 375° in a deep fat fryer or other deep, heavy pot.

Stir buttermilk and scallions into the cornmeal mixture, then stir in the egg. Slip the batter by the heaping tablespoonful into the oil. Do not crowd the pan.

Cook the hush puppies until they are a deep golden brown, turning once or twice. Drain them on paper towels and keep in a warm place. After all the hush puppies have been cooked, serve them hot.

Nearly 45 percent of Maryland is farmland, cultivated for produce, corn, and soybeans.

SWEET POTATO BREAD

MAKES ONE 9 × 5-INCH LOAF, OR THREE 3 × 5-INCH
LOAVES

  1 medium sweet potato, about 8 ounces
1½ cups unbleached white flour
  ¾ teaspoon baking powder
  ½ teaspoon baking soda
  ½ teaspoon salt
  ½ teaspoon ground mace
  ¼ teaspoon ground cinnamon
  ¾ cup sugar
  ⅓ cup unsalted butter, softened
  2 extra large eggs, separated
  ¼ cup milk
  ½ teaspoon pure vanilla extract
  ½ cup chopped pecans or walnuts

Cut the sweet potato in half lengthwise and steam it in its jacket until tender, about 20 minutes. Scoop out the meat and puree it. You should have about 1 cup of puree.

Butter pans and preheat the oven to 350°.

Sift the flour, baking powder, baking soda, salt, and spices together. Cream the sugar and butter in a mixer and beat in the egg yolks. With a wooden spoon, stir in the sweet potato puree, milk, and vanilla. Fold in the chopped nuts. Fold in the flour in 3 or 4 additions; do not overmix.

Beat the egg whites until stiff but not dry. Add about one-third of the beaten whites to lighten the batter, then fold in the rest of the whites in two batches.

Turn the batter into the prepared pans. Bake for 45 to 50 minutes for small pans, or 55 minutes to an hour for a large pan, until a cake tester inserted in the center comes out clean. Cool in the pans on a rack for about 5 minutes, then either turn the bread out to cool completely, or serve it warm.

CORN MUFFINS

White cornmeal, called for in this recipe, has a sweeter, more delicate flavor than yellow cornmeal. Yellow cornmeal may be substituted; when we use it, we often replace the sugar with molasses for a heartier, heavier-textured muffin.

MAKES 1 DOZEN MUFFINS

1¼ cups white cornmeal
1 cup unbleached white flour
2 teaspoons baking powder
¾ teaspoon salt
2 tablespoons sugar
2 extra large eggs, lightly beaten
¼ cup vegetable or corn oil
1¼ cups milk
Molasses (optional)

Preheat the oven to 400° and butter a muffin tin. Combine the dry ingredients in a bowl and stir with a wooden spoon to blend. Mix the liquid ingredients together in a small bowl. Pour into the dry ingredients and stir just until blended.

Spoon the batter evenly into the buttered muffin tin, filling each cup about three-quarters full. Bake for about 20 minutes or just until the tops of the muffins are a light golden brown. Remove from pan and serve immediately with butter, and with molasses if desired.

THREE-WAY SPOON BREAD

"Three-way" because this bread uses cornmeal, grits, and fresh corn, giving it a goodly amount of texture and flavor.

SERVES 6 TO 8

½ cup yellow cornmeal
½ cup grits
2 cups water
1½ teaspoons salt
2½ tablespoons unsalted butter
Approximately ¾ cup fresh corn kernels, cut from 1 medium ear of corn
1 cup milk
2 extra large eggs, lightly beaten
Freshly ground black pepper or pinch of cayenne (optional)

Stir the cornmeal and grits into the water in a saucepan. Add ½ teaspoon of the salt. Bring to a simmer over low heat, stirring constantly, and continue cooking for 5 minutes.

Transfer the cooked cornmeal to a bowl and stir in 2 tablespoons of the butter, letting the butter melt and cooling the mixture a bit.

Preheat the oven to 375°. Lightly butter an 8-inch-square baking dish with the remaining ½ tablespoon of butter.

Add the rest of the salt, the fresh corn, and the milk to the cornmeal mixture and stir well. Add the eggs to the mixture and blend them in well. Season with black pepper or cayenne if desired.

Pour the batter into the prepared baking dish and bake 35 to 40 minutes, until the spoon bread is puffy and a rich golden brown on top. Serve hot.

Corn, both feed corn for animals and delicious Silver Queen sweet white corn for the table, is a leading crop in Delaware and Maryland.

CHESAPEAKE CHEESE STRAWS

Every so often, we succumb to the urge to eat some good homemade junk food. These cheese straws satisfy that urge perfectly—they are well seasoned, but not as salty as commercial nibbles, though they are rich. Most of our guests find them irresistible. The recipe can be easily doubled.

SERVES 4 TO 5; APPROXIMATELY 3 DOZEN STRAWS

1 cup unbleached white flour
2 teaspoons Chesapeake seafood seasoning
⅛ teaspoon cayenne
4 tablespoons unsalted butter, softened
1 extra large egg, lightly beaten
3 tablespoons cold water
4 ounces aged cheddar, finely grated

Sift the flour with the seafood seasoning and cayenne. Cut butter into the flour to make a fine meal. Blend in the egg and water. Stir in the cheese.

Roll the dough between wax paper to a ¼-inch thickness. Chill 30 minutes or longer. Preheat the oven to 425°.

Remove the top sheet of wax paper and with a sharp knife cut the dough into straws ¼ inch thick and about 3 inches long. Invert the cut straws back onto the top sheet of wax paper for ease in removing them. Transfer the straws to ungreased baking sheets, placing them about ½ inch apart.

Bake the straws for 8 to 10 minutes, until pale golden brown and bubbly. Serve hot in a basket or on a tray lined with a napkin.

BROWN BREAD WITH ONION AND CURRANTS

These round loaves are a hybrid pumpernickel-dark rye. We prefer the flavor of currants, but raisins may be substituted. The bread is flavorful and nutritious, good with soups and stews, and it makes delicious ham or cream cheese sandwiches.

MAKES 2 LARGE ROUND LOAVES

2 tablespoons active dry yeast
1 cup warm water with a pinch of sugar
1 cup milk, scalded and cooled to lukewarm
¼ cup molasses
½ cup strong coffee
¼ cup vegetable oil
2 teaspoons salt
2 cups rye flour
1 cup bran
1½ cups whole wheat flour
1½ cups unbleached white flour, plus ½ to ¾ cup for kneading
⅓ cup currants, soaked, then squeezed of excess water
⅓ cup finely minced onion
1 extra large egg beaten with 1 teaspoon water
Cornmeal

Stir the yeast into the warm water; let proof until foamy. Meanwhile, combine the milk, molasses, coffee, and oil in a large bowl. When the yeast is foamy, stir it into the liquid ingredients.

Mix the salt with the rye flour and stir it into the liquid ingredients with a wooden spoon. Add the bran and stir well. Add the whole wheat and unbleached flours, about a cup at a time, blending well after each addition. When the dough becomes too stiff to stir, turn it onto a floured work surface.

Knead the dough for 5 to 10 minutes, adding a little flour as necessary so that the dough does not stick to the surface. The dough will be slightly sticky. Place the dough in a lightly oiled bowl and cover with plastic wrap or a slightly dampened tea towel.

Let the dough rise in a warm place for about 2 hours or until it has doubled in bulk. (Or let the dough rise in the refrigerator overnight. This gives a better yeast distribution and better structure to this heavy dough. About 4 hours before baking the bread, remove the dough from the refrigerator and let it sit in a warm place for 2 or 3 hours before kneading in the currants and onions.)

Punch down the dough and divide it in half. Flatten one portion to a ¾-inch thickness and sprinkle one-quarter of the currants and onions over the dough. Fold the dough in half and gently knead in the currants and onions. Flatten the dough again to about a ¾-inch thickness, add another quarter of the currants and onions, and knead. Form the dough into a round loaf. Repeat this process with the other half of the dough and the remaining currants and onions.

Preheat oven to 350°, with a baking stone if you have one. If you are using a baking stone, place the loaves on baker's paddles sprinkled lightly with cornmeal. Or place loaves on a lightly greased baking sheet sprinkled lightly with cornmeal. Cover the loaves loosely with a slightly dampened tea towel and let rise in a warm place for about 40 minutes or until doubled in bulk.

Brush the loaves all over generously with the egg and water. Place the baking sheet in the oven or slide the loaves onto the preheated stone. Bake for 1 hour, remove from oven, and place on racks to cool.

STOLLEN

By using ricotta in this recipe you don't need the large amounts of butter and eggs usually required for stollen. Keep the stollen wrapped in parchment or wax paper at room temperature; this gives the crust the customary dryness. We also like the bread toasted and serve it for Christmas and New Year's Day breakfasts.

MAKES 1 LARGE OR 2 SMALL STOLLEN

1½ tablespoons active dry yeast
⅓ cup warm water
 1 pound unbleached white flour or bread flour, about 4 cups
 1 teaspoon baking powder
½ teaspoon salt
¼ teaspoon cinnamon
¼ teaspoon freshly grated nutmeg
¼ teaspoon cardamom
¼ teaspoon ground cloves
¼ cup currants
¼ cup dark rum or brandy
 4 ounces dried apricots
¼ pound unsalted butter, softened
½ cup sugar
½ pound ricotta
 2 extra large eggs
 4 ounces blanched almonds, coarsely chopped
   Grated zest of 1 orange
   Grated zest of 1 lemon
 2 tablespoons unsalted butter, melted
½ cup sifted confectioners' sugar (optional)

Stir the yeast into the warm water and let it proof until it is foamy. Meanwhile, sift the flour, baking powder, salt, and spices together. Soak the currants in the rum or brandy to soften them. Soak the apricots in warm water to soften them. Drain the currants and apricots well and pat dry. Chop the apricots coarsely.

Cream the butter with the sugar. Mix in the ricotta. Add the eggs to this mixture, one at a time, and stir well after each addition.

Gradually add about half the flour to the butter-ricotta mixture, incorporating well. Stir in the yeast, then mix in the remaining flour. Turn the dough onto a lightly floured board and knead in the almonds, currants, apricots, and citrus zest. Knead in a little more flour if the dough is sticky. It should be soft and tender.

Let the dough rise in a lightly greased bowl until doubled in bulk, about 3 hours. Or cover the bowl tightly and let rise overnight in the refrigerator; bring the dough to room temperature before shaping for baking.

When ready to bake, punch down the dough and roll it into a 9 × 15-inch oval. Fold it in half lengthwise and let rise on a greased baking sheet until almost doubled in bulk. Or shape the dough into two smaller stollen and place each on a separate baking sheet to rise.

While the dough is rising, preheat the oven to 375°. Bake the stollen on the baking sheet(s) for 45 to 50 minutes, until it turns a rich, deep golden brown. Brush all over with the melted butter while the stollen is still very warm. Cool on a rack and sprinkle with confectioners' sugar if desired.

GINNY GLENN'S ANGEL BISCUITS

Mrs. Ginny Glenn of Milford, Delaware, has lived in and collected recipes from several Chesapeake locations. These biscuits are an adaptation of her mother's Tidewater Virginia recipe. Leavened with both yeast and baking powder, they are very light, thus their name. Cooks in the Chesapeake region often use buttermilk in quick breads; it seems to make the breads lighter and more flavorful.

MAKES APPROXIMATELY 18 2½-INCH BISCUITS, OR 30 1½-INCH BISCUITS

  1 tablespoon active dry yeast
  ¼ cup warm water
2½ cups unbleached white flour
  1 teaspoon baking powder
  2 teaspoons sugar
  1 teaspoon salt
  ½ cup vegetable shortening
  1 cup buttermilk

Stir the yeast into the warm water and let it proof until foamy. Combine the dry ingredients in a mixing bowl. Cut in the shortening to make a medium-fine meal. Add the buttermilk and yeast mixture and mix well. Turn the dough onto a lightly floured board and knead lightly. The dough will be soft but should not be sticky.

Place the dough in a lightly oiled bowl, cover with plastic wrap, and let rise in the refrigerator overnight. The dough may be allowed to rise until doubled in bulk at room temperature, but the baked biscuits will not rise as much.

Preheat the oven to 400°. Punch down the dough, cover, and let it rest for 10 to 15 minutes. Turn it onto a floured surface and roll to ½-inch thickness. Cut with a 2½-inch or 1½-inch biscuit cutter. Place the biscuits on lightly greased baking sheets and bake for about 18 minutes, until pale golden brown on top and deep golden brown on the bottom.

CORNMEAL WAFFLES

These waffles are crisp on the outside and tender on the inside and have a rich cornmeal flavor. They are deliciously accented by the fruity flavor of Blackberry Syrup (page 171).

MAKES ABOUT 6 LARGE WAFFLES

  ½ cup unbleached white flour
  ½ cup whole wheat pastry flour
  1 cup yellow stone-ground cornmeal
  3 teaspoons baking powder
  ½ teaspoon salt
  2 extra large eggs, separated
  2 cups milk
  ⅔ cup vegetable or corn oil

Heat the waffle iron. Combine all the dry ingredients and sift into a mixing bowl. In a small bowl, combine the egg yolks, milk, and oil, and blend well.

Beat the egg whites until stiff. Pour the liquid ingredients into the dry and stir well. Fold the egg whites into the batter. Cook the waffles in a lightly oiled, hot waffle iron according to the manufacturer's instructions. Serve immediately.

This restored 19th-century church, left, now serves as both art gallery and dwelling.

Flowers are sold by home gardeners at roadside farm stands on the honor system: "take a bouquet and put your money in the jar."

CORN PONE

Corn pone, which used to be served in the Chesapeake as a one-dish breakfast, is a fine accompaniment to baked or fried ham, or pork chops. It has a light and custardy texture, similar to that of spoon bread. Cold leftover corn pone may be sliced and fried in butter or bacon drippings, but care must be taken in turning the slices so they don't crumble.

SERVES 4 TO 6

1½ cups stone-ground yellow cornmeal
  2 cups water
  ¼ cup melted unsalted butter plus ½ tablespoon
     softened butter or vegetable shortening
     Scant teaspoon salt
  1 teaspoon baking soda
  1 cup buttermilk, or 1 cup milk mixed with
     1 tablespoon vinegar
  2 eggs, beaten
  2 or 3 ounces pork cracklings, or diced and
     fried bacon (optional)

Stir the cornmeal and water together in a saucepan and place over low heat. Stir constantly while you bring the mixture to a simmer and cook for 5 minutes. Turn the mixture into a bowl and stir in the butter or shortening and salt.

Preheat the oven to 400°. Butter a 1½-quart baking dish generously with ½ tablespoon of butter.

Mix the baking soda with the buttermilk or milk-vinegar and stir into the cornmeal. Beat the eggs into the mixture one at a time. Stir in the cracklings or bacon, if you are using.

Turn the batter into the baking dish and bake for about 30 minutes, or until golden brown. Serve hot.

WIMPY'S FRENCH TOAST

Ocean City, Maryland, is a large resort area that employs thousands of teenagers every summer. In her youth, Susan spent a summer waitressing there, working in a coffeeshop that was well known for its breakfasts. Wimpy was the jolly, portly cook, and he gave her his recipe for french toast. It has withstood our recipe test for years. Wimpy made it with white bread, but we prefer it with whole wheat. His reminder: "Be sure your griddle is good and hot."

SERVES 2

  1 extra large egg, beaten
  ½ cup milk
  1 teaspoon sugar
     Few pinches salt
  ½ teaspoon cinnamon
  ¼ teaspoon pure vanilla extract
  2 tablespoons vegetable oil
  4 slices whole wheat bread

GARNISH: pure maple syrup, confectioners' sugar, or jam

Put all ingredients except the bread in a shallow dish and mix very well with a fork. Heat a griddle with just a little oil until hot.

Dip one side of each slice of bread in the egg mixture, turn with a fork or tongs to dip the other side, and place on the hot griddle. Pour the remaining egg mixture over the slices.

Cook over medium heat until the toast is well browned on one side, about 4 minutes. Turn and cook until the other side is well browned. Serve immediately on warm plates with butter and maple syrup, confectioners' sugar, or jam.

YEASTED BUCKWHEAT CAKES

The sponge for these pancakes must be made the night before. The egg, baking soda, and hot water are added the following morning.

MAKES 16 4-INCH CAKES

  2 cups milk
  1 tablespoon dark brown sugar
  1 tablespoon active dry yeast
  3 tablespoons vegetable oil
1¼ cups buckwheat
1¼ cups unbleached white flour
  1 teaspoon salt
  1 extra large egg, lightly beaten
  ½ teaspoon baking soda
  ⅓ tablespoon hot water
     Maple syrup

Heat the milk to lukewarm, add the sugar, and stir until it dissolves. Add the yeast, stir, and let sit until foamy, about 5 minutes. Stir in the vegetable oil.

Blend the buckwheat and white flour with the salt. Add to the milk mixture, about ½ cup at a time, stirring well after each addition. Cover the bowl with plastic wrap and place in the refrigerator or in a very cool place overnight.

Remove the batter from the refrigerator and let sit at least 30 minutes. Beat the egg into the batter. Dissolve the baking soda in the hot water, stir into the batter, and blend well. Let the batter rise in a warm place for 30 minutes.

Pour about ⅓ cup batter for each cake onto a hot, lightly oiled griddle and cook for 2 to 3 minutes on each side or until golden brown. Serve hot with butter and maple syrup.

STICKY BUNS

The dough for these buns should be placed in the refrigerator to rise overnight. Bake the buns in the morning and serve warm for breakfast.

MAKES 12 LARGE BUNS

DOUGH

¾ cup milk
5 tablespoons unsalted butter, cut into 5 pieces
1 tablespoon active dry yeast
1 teaspoon plus ¼ cup sugar
2 tablespoons warm water
2 extra large eggs, beaten
¾ teaspoon salt
3 cups unbleached white flour, plus ½ cup for kneading

FILLING

2 tablespoons sugar
½ teaspoon cinnamon
A few generous grindings of nutmeg
⅓ cup coarsely chopped pecans

TOPPING

½ cup light brown sugar
½ cup light honey
6 tablespoons unsalted butter
½ teaspoon cinnamon
¼ teaspoon mace
⅛ teaspoon freshly ground nutmeg
¾ cup coarsely ground pecans

Scald the milk, remove it from the heat, stir in the butter and set aside. In a cup, combine the yeast, 1 teaspoon of the sugar, and the warm water and let stand until the yeast is foamy, about 5 minutes. When the milk and butter mixture has cooled to lukewarm, beat in the eggs, the remaining ¼ cup sugar, and the salt.

Put 3 cups of flour in a large bowl and make a well in it. Pour the milk and the yeast mixtures into the well. Stir with a wooden spoon until the liquids and all of the flour are well incorporated.

Turn the dough out onto a floured pastry board or a marble. Knead for about 4 minutes, adding flour as needed. The dough should be slightly sticky. Put the dough into a lightly oiled bowl, cover tightly with plastic wrap, and place in the refrigerator or a cool place overnight.

If the dough has been refrigerated, allow it to come to cool room temperature. Butter two 8-inch round baking pans. Knead the dough for a few minutes, then flatten into a long rectangle, about 8 × 15 inches.

Make the filling by mixing the sugar with the cinnamon. Sprinkle the mixture over the dough, grate a bit of nutmeg over this, and scatter the pecans over the top. Gently but firmly roll the dough up lengthwise into a long cylinder.

For the topping, combine the light brown sugar, honey, and butter in a heavy-bottomed skillet and melt quickly over medium-low heat, stirring occasionally. Stir in the remaining spices and nuts. Pour half of the mixture into each prepared baking pan.

Preheat the oven to 350°. Cut the cylinder into 12 fat slices, 1 to 1½ inches wide. Place 6 slices, cut side up, in each pan. Cover the pans lightly with a damp tea towel and let the dough rise for about 20 minutes, or until almost doubled in bulk.

Bake the buns for 20 to 23 minutes, until they are a rich golden brown. Remove from the oven and invert each pan onto a platter to turn out the buns. Scrape any topping that has stuck to the pan onto the buns. Let the buns cool for at least 15 or 20 minutes before serving. Serve warm or at room temperature.

SOUPS
AND
CHOWDERS

oup of the evening, beautiful soup!" Beautiful soup was turtle to Lewis Carroll but is terrapin in the Chesapeake region. The name terrapin originated with the Algonquin Delaware Indians, as did the name Chesapeake itself. The old-world immigrants seized upon the terrapin as a great delicacy; it is mentioned in most recipe collections of the eighteenth and nineteenth centuries, when it was eaten by the upper classes, and was the *pièce de résistance* of banquets.

Today, with both lavish banquets and the market for turtle in decline, the preferred soups are crab, chicken, and chowder, the kinds of hearty soups that have nourished and gladdened generations of Chesapeake natives. Vegetables figure copiously, testimony to their availability and the goodness of the land. Ham, bacon, and salt pork are frequent enrichments. However long the ingredients lists, definite traditions of soup-making render these soups well thought out rather than the results of pantry searches. They are flavorful, exuberant dishes, characterized by the region's agricultural history and proximity to water, with the land and Bay concentrated in the kettle.

Chesapeake cooks have always considered soup and chowder important sustenance. For the poor, soup was usually the basis of a meal. For the better off, it was the start of a meal, and a good way to use the still protein-rich bones and leftover bits of poultry, game, beef, lamb, and pork. Frugality in the kitchen was a virtue that was especially rewarded by the great flavor of fresh and well-made stocks and broths.

Oddly, for a region with such a variety of fish, fish stock or *fumet* has never been featured much. In the early manor houses such as Jefferson's and Washington's, cooks followed the French custom of adding wine to fish and shellfish soups. By the time the Republic was established, dairy herds were commonplace and most people adapted the English and Breton usage of milk and cream in chowders. Chicken, ham, beef, or veal broth are the soup bases used today, even for seafood soups.

The soup recipes that have been handed down from generation to generation are associated with particular geographic areas. On the Peninsula and in the Jewish communities of the region, chicken soups are specialties. Many cooks in Delaware and on the Eastern Shore add Slippery Dumplings—a kind of noodle—and vegetables to their chicken soups. Gloria Greene, a Maryland resident and food writer, tells us that Jewish cooks usually add matzo balls, but sometimes enrich the soup with home-made egg noodles. Her mother also freezes leftover bits of meat to fill the noodles that she adds to her chicken soup. In Tidewater Virginia, southern Maryland, and Delaware, ham or ham hocks remain the choice for flavoring soups made with greens, mixed vegetables, or beans, while vegetables are the basis of many soups in mainland Maryland, especially Baltimore, Annapolis, and Howard County. Wholesome and tasty ham and vegetable soups also figure prominently on the weekly menus of many black families. Dorothy Smith, of Howard County, remembers that as a girl she helped her mother and grandmother can mixed vegetables for winter soups.

The great soups of the Chesapeake, however, by virtue of their popularity and the number of variations, are crab soups, the most widely favored being Maryland crab soup. It may be very dense, almost like gumbo, though we do not think it is best in this form. It is always complex, with beef stock and bacon to give it body, a garden's worth of vegetables for interest and color, crab for sweetness, and spices for spark. It is an informal party and family gathering soup, appreciated by crab lovers who feel at home picking crab from the shells. Cream of crab soup, on the other hand, represents finesse, with the crabmeat already picked, a base of chicken broth rather than beef stock, additions of cream and butter, a discreet amount of vegetables, and an elegant garnish of sherry. For many natives, she-crab soup, made whenever an egg-bearing female crab can be obtained, is the finest. The eggs are stirred into either Maryland crab soup or an ultra version of cream of crab.

Although there are fewer variations of other soups, family cooks rely on tradition and ingenuity to guide them through a complete soup repertoire. Repetition is not shunned; soup is a comforting food, and many people enjoy the small ritual of the same soup every Friday. For a change of pace, however, someone in a Chesapeake kitchen can usually be counted on to have a good idea, such as adding Slippery Dumplings to soup made with ham and lima beans rather than with the usual chicken.

ALMA'S MARYLAND CRAB SOUP

This recipe, which belonged to Susan's paternal grandmother, who was a native Marylander, comes to us from Susan's Uncle Parker, who keeps the tradition alive. He usually doubles this recipe for family gatherings.

SERVES 8 TO 10
MAKES APPROXIMATELY 1 GALLON SOUP

3 tablespoons vegetable or olive oil
1½ pounds chuck roast, trimmed and cut into 1-inch cubes
½ cup all-purpose flour
8 ounces bacon, cut into 1-inch pieces
3 bay leaves
1¼ quarts water
1 pound Maryland crabmeat
4 whole steamed Maryland hard crabs
1½ pounds fresh tomatoes, peeled, or canned tomatoes
1 medium yellow onion, diced
1 quart beef broth
2 cups corn kernels, cut from 3 or 4 fresh ears
¾ cup small-dice carrots, 1 large or 2 small carrots
1 cup shelled lima beans or 1 cup green beans, cut into 1½-inch pieces (optional)
1 cup shelled peas, approximately ¾ pound unshelled peas
Chesapeake seafood seasoning to taste

Heat the oil in a large soup kettle. Dust the meat cubes with flour. Add the meat to the hot oil in batches and brown evenly. When all the meat has been browned, add the bacon, bay leaves, and the water. Bring to a boil, cover, and simmer for 1 hour. Skim the fat off the top occasionally. Meanwhile, remove the cartilage from the crabmeat. Remove the aprons, top shells, and gills from the steamed crabs and quarter them. Set crabmeat and crabs aside.

Add the tomatoes, onion, and beef broth to the soup and simmer for 15 to 20 minutes. Add the corn and carrots and lima beans or green beans. Simmer for 15 to 20 minutes. Add the peas, crabmeat, and steamed crabs. Simmer for about 10 minutes; add seasoning to taste. Bring the soup to a vigorous simmer for 10 minutes. Serve hot.

Note: This soup freezes fairly well, but it is chancy to refrigerate it, especially in hot weather. It is best made just before serving. Or make it beforehand and cool it to room temperature; then pack it in freezer containers and freeze immediately. Susan's grandmother used to freeze it in bread loaf pans. To reheat, put the frozen blocks of soup in a large pot and simmer slowly until it is very hot. If you can find the mature she-crabs, you will have the delicious roe to enrich the soup.

SIMPLE CRAB SOUP

SERVES 4 TO 6

2 tablespoons vegetable oil
1 medium carrot, diced
½ medium onion, diced
2 quarts chicken broth
1 pound potatoes, peeled and cut in ½-inch cubes
1 pound ripe tomatoes, peeled, seeded, and diced, or canned tomatoes, drained
2 teaspoons Chesapeake seafood seasoning, or to taste
1 pound Maryland crabmeat, cartilage removed
About 2 tablespoons chopped parsley

Place the oil in a soup pot, and add the carrots and onions. Cover the pot and cook the vegetables over low heat just until softened. Add the broth, potatoes, tomatoes, and seafood seasoning. Simmer just until the potatoes are tender, about 10 minutes. Add the crabmeat and parsley and heat through. Serve hot.

CREAM OF CRAB SOUP

After testing many recipes for Cream of Crab Soup, we think this one equals the best restaurant soup we have tasted, that of the Narrows Restaurant at Kent Narrows on the Eastern Shore of Maryland.

SERVES 4 TO 6

1 pound lump, backfin, or regular crabmeat
¼ cup grated onion
1 medium carrot, grated
2 tablespoons unsalted butter
2 tablespoons all-purpose flour
2 cups chicken broth
2 cups half-and-half
1 tablespoon dry sherry
1 or 2 dashes of Tabasco
　Salt

GARNISH: 1 tablespoon chopped parsley
　　　　　dry sherry

Remove any cartilage from the crabmeat and set the crab aside. In a soup pot, soften the onion and carrot in the butter over low heat. After the vegetables have cooked for about 10 minutes, sprinkle them with the flour and cook for about 5 minutes, being careful the flour does not brown.

Stir in the chicken broth and the half-and-half. Add the sherry and Tabasco. Cook, stirring occasionally, for about 10 minutes. Add the crabmeat and heat thoroughly for about 5 minutes. Adjust the seasoning.

Serve the soup garnished with the chopped parsley and pass a pitcher of sherry.

SOFT SHELL CLAM CHOWDER

SERVES 4 TO 6

6 dozen soft shell clams
⅓ cup cornmeal
3 cups water
¼ pound bacon
1 medium onion, diced
1½ pounds potatoes, peeled and diced
2 sprigs fresh savory, or ½ teaspoon dried savory leaves
½ teaspoon Chesapeake seafood seasoning

Scrub the clams well with a brush. Place in a large bowl and cover with approximately 1 inch of water. Sprinkle the cornmeal, which activates the cleansing process, over the water and let the clams stand for 30 minutes or longer. Drain and rinse under cold running water.

Put the clams in a large pot with a tight-fitting lid. Add ½ cup of water and steam the clams just until they open, about 5 minutes. Let them cool and remove them from the shells; discard the necks. Strain the broth through finely woven cheesecloth or paper toweling. If the clams are very sandy, rinse them in the broth and strain the broth again. There should be about 2 cups of broth. Reserve the clams and the broth.

Fry the bacon until it is crisp. Drain on paper towels. Remove all but about 2 tablespoons of the fat from the pan. Add the diced onion to the fat and heat to soften the onion. When the onion is golden, add the diced potatoes and cook for 5 minutes.

Transfer the vegetables to a soup pot. Taste the broth for saltiness. If it is very salty, add only about two-thirds of it to the vegetables at this time. Add 2 or 3 cups of water to the pot, depending on the saltiness of the broth. Add the savory and the seafood seasoning. Bring the soup to a simmer and cook until the potatoes are barely tender, about 8 minutes.

Cook the soup another few minutes, until the potatoes are done. Adjust the seasoning, adding more broth if necessary. Serve the soup very hot. Just before serving, crumble the bacon and sprinkle on the soup as a garnish.

An aerial view of Oxford shows the close relationship of land, water, and community, typical of Maryland's Eastern Shore.

LOBSTER BISQUE

In this frugal lobster bisque, adapted from Fifty Years in a Maryland Kitchen *by Mrs. B. C. Howard, only the claw and body meat, and coral if available, are put into the soup. The tail meat is reserved for salads. The bisque doesn't taste frugal; we find it rich indeed.*

SERVES 4 TO 8

2 to 4 cooked lobsters, totaling 3½ to 4 pounds
1 medium onion, chopped
1 medium celery rib, chopped
1 medium carrot, chopped
1 anchovy fillet
½ cup dry white wine
1 teaspoon sea or kosher salt
1 teaspoon black peppercorns
1 blade mace, or ¼ teaspoon ground mace
2 tablespoons unsalted butter
¼ cup grated onion
2 tablespoons all-purpose flour
1 cup half-and-half
1 cup milk
3 cups lobster-shell broth
   Salt and freshly ground white pepper
   Pinch cayenne pepper
1 tablespoon cognac (optional)

GARNISH: paprika

Remove the meat from the lobster shells. Reserve the tail meat for another use. Dice the body and claw meat and refrigerate until ready to use.

Crush the lobster shells and place in a stockpot with the onion, celery, carrot, anchovy, white wine, salt, peppercorns, and mace. Add water to barely cover. Simmer the broth for 45 minutes, skimming as necessary. Strain the broth through rinsed cheese-cloth in a fine strainer. There should be about 1 quart of broth. Taste the broth; if it is very mild, reduce over medium heat by about one-quarter.

Melt the butter in a soup pot over medium-low heat and soften the grated onion in it for about 10 minutes. Sprinkle the flour over the onion and cook for about 5 minutes, being careful that the flour does not brown.

Stir in the half-and-half, milk, and 3 cups lobster broth. Refrigerate or freeze the remaining broth for another soup or sauce. Season the soup with salt, white and cayenne pepper, and cook for 10 minutes, stirring occasionally. Stir in the lobster meat and add the cognac at this time, if desired. Heat the soup on low-simmer for about 5 minutes. Serve the soup very hot and garnish it with a dusting of paprika.

RICH CHICKEN BROTH

The best broth will be made with a stewing hen, preferably with the feet still attached. Remove the feet or have the butcher do it for you. Scrub the feet well before adding them to the pot. If you cannot find a stewing hen, use 6 pounds of backs and necks, and any leftover—cooked or uncooked—chicken bones. Hearts and gizzards are fine to add to the pot in small amounts, but do not use any livers, as these impart a bitter taste to the broth. The hen will release most of its flavor to the broth, but the meat may be used in a salad or pot pie.

MAKES 2 QUARTS BROTH

1   4-pound stewing hen
2   pounds chicken backs and necks, or 2 pounds leftover wing tips, other pieces, or bones from cooked chicken
1   medium onion, peeled and coarsely chopped
1   medium carrot, peeled and coarsely chopped
1   medium celery rib, peeled and coarsely chopped
1   bay leaf
1   teaspoon black peppercorns

Rinse uncooked chicken and remove extra fat. Place it in a 10-quart stockpot with all the chicken bones and cover with cold water. Bring just to a boil. Skim the broth and reduce the heat. Simmer the broth for an hour, skimming occasionally.

Add the onion, carrot, celery, bay leaf, and peppercorns to the stockpot. Simmer for 1½ hours, skimming occasionally. Taste the broth—it should be well flavored; if not, simmer it for another 30 minutes.

Strain the broth through a colander lined with rinsed fine-weave cheesecloth. Cool to room temperature, then store in the refrigerator or freezer. The broth may be refrigerated for 5 days. Bring to a rolling boil for 5 minutes before using. It will keep in the freezer for 6 months, but will have the best flavor during the first 2 months.

CHICKEN AND SLIPPERY DUMPLINGS

This is a Delaware and Eastern Shore specialty. Mrs. Ginny Glenn, whose dumpling recipe we have adapted, tells us that a favorite Delaware variation is to simmer ham hocks until they are tender, then cook the dumplings and shelled fresh peas in the stock. Fresh lima beans are also paired with slippery dumplings, with either ham or chicken. The dumplings are really a type of noodle, rather than raised dumplings.

SERVES 6 TO 8

DUMPLINGS

2   cups unbleached white flour
1   teaspoon salt
¼   cup vegetable oil
½   cup plus 3 tablespoons ice water

CHICKEN

1   4- to 5-pound fryer or stewing chicken
½   medium onion
2   quarts chicken broth
4 or 5 parsley sprigs
1   bay leaf
½   teaspoon dried thyme leaves
1   teaspoon black peppercorns
    Salt and freshly ground black pepper
2   medium carrots, diced
½   medium onion, diced
1 or 2 tablespoons flour (optional)
1 to 1½ cups shelled peas

GARNISH: chopped parsley

Make the dumplings first. They keep well refrigerated on baking sheets covered with tea towels. Do not lay the dumplings on top of one another.

The dumplings may be made by hand or in a food processor. By hand, mix the flour and salt together in a bowl. Add the oil and ½ cup of the water. Stir quickly and add extra water if the mixture is dry. The dough will be mealy when mixed, but should clump into a stiff dough when a handful is squeezed in the fist. Add more water, a tablespoon at a time, if the dough is still dry.

Turn the dough onto a work surface and knead it into a firm mass. This is easier if you divide the loose dough into two portions and knead one at a time. Let the dough rest, covered with plastic or under an over-turned bowl, for at least 30 minutes.

If using a food processor, pulse the flour and salt to mix. With the machine running, quickly add the vegetable oil and all the water through the feed tube. Process just enough to mix. Turn the dough onto a work surface, knead, and let it rest as above.

Roll the dough very thin, about 1/16 inch thick, with a rolling pin or through a pasta machine. Cut the dough into rectangles about 1½ × 2½ inches. The dumplings may be stored in the refrigerator at this point; they improve in texture if made a day ahead and stored.

Rinse and pat the chicken dry; remove any extra fat. Place the half onion in the chicken cavity. Truss the chicken.

Place the chicken, breast up, in a large stewpot, casserole, or Dutch oven. Add the broth; it should come about halfway up the chicken. Add a little water if necessary. Tie the herbs and peppercorns in cheese-cloth and add to the pot. Salt lightly if the broth is unsalted.

Cover and cook at a simmer about 1 hour and 10 minutes, turning the chicken twice so the breast is facing up at the end of the cooking. Add the diced carrots and onion to the pan about 15 minutes before the chicken is done. If you wish to thicken the broth, remove about ½ cup of broth before you add the carrots and onions. Let the broth cool, mix in the flour if you want it thickened, and set aside.

When the chicken is cooked, remove it to a plat-ter. Remove the herbs. Spoon a little broth over the chicken and cover it loosely with foil. Keep it warm in a low oven.

After the carrots and onions have cooked about 15 minutes, carefully add the dumplings to the broth, stirring with a wooden fork or spoon. Then add the peas and flour-broth mixture to thicken the soup. Stir the soup occasionally while the dumplings cook. The dumplings take between 5 and 8 minutes to cook, depending on how long ahead they have been made. Season with salt and freshly ground pepper to taste.

Serve the dumplings and broth as a first course. Reserve a little broth to serve with the chicken as a second course. Garnish the chicken with chopped parsley.

VEGETABLE CORN CHOWDER

SERVES 6

  2 tablespoons unsalted butter
  2 tablespoons olive or vegetable oil
  1 medium onion, chopped
  ¾ pound new potatoes, scrubbed and cut into
     ½-inch dice
  4 cups vegetable or light chicken stock
  1 bay leaf
  ¾ teaspoon fresh chopped thyme, or ¼
     teaspoon dried thyme, crumbled
  ¾ teaspoon fresh chopped marjoram, or
     ¼ teaspoon dried marjoram, crumbled
  2 cups yellow corn kernels, fresh or frozen
     (unthawed)
  2 cups baby lima beans, fresh or frozen
     (unthawed)
1½ cups half-and-half
1½ teaspoons Chesapeake seafood seasoning, or
     to taste
     Salt and freshly ground black pepper to taste

Heat the butter and oil in a soup pot over low heat. Soften the onion in it for about 5 minutes. Stir in the potatoes, cover, and cook for 5 to 7 minutes, stirring occasionally. Stir in the stock and herbs, cover, and bring to a simmer. Cook for about 5 minutes.

Add the fresh corn and lima beans and cook for 10 to 12 minutes. (If you use frozen corn and lima beans, cook only 6 to 8 minutes.)

Stir in the half-and-half and the seafood seasoning and cook for a few minutes. Taste for salt and pep-per; the seafood seasoning is spicy and contains salt, so adjust salt and pepper carefully.

Puree half of the soup in a blender in batches. Return the pureed soup to the soup pot and heat over low heat for about 5 minutes. Taste for seasoning and serve hot.

EARLY AUTUMN VEGETABLE CHOWDER

SERVES 4 TO 6

1 large sweet red pepper
1 large sweet yellow pepper
4 medium leeks
2 tablespoons unsalted butter
2 tablespoons olive or vegetable oil
1 medium potato
2 cups vegetable or light chicken stock
1 pound tomatoes, peeled
  Salt and freshly ground black pepper
1½ cups half-and-half

Halve the peppers lengthwise and seed them. Place cut side down on a foil-covered broiler tray and broil just long enough to blister the skins. When the peppers are blackened, place them in a paper bag for about 5 minutes, then remove the skins.

Wash and trim the leeks, leaving about ½ inch of green. Halve the leeks lengthwise and rinse well. Slice them crosswise thin.

Heat the butter and oil in a soup pot over low heat and add the leeks. Cover and sweat them for about 20 minutes. Meanwhile, peel the potato and grate it fine. Add the potato to the leeks, cover the pot, and cook for another 5 minutes. Stir in the stock.

Cut the peppers into bite-size pieces, add to the soup, and cook for about 5 minutes. Puree the tomatoes and add to the soup. Season the soup with salt and pepper and cook for about 5 minutes.

Puree half of the soup and return it to the pot. Stir in the half-and-half and heat thoroughly but do not boil. Taste for seasoning and serve the soup hot.

WINTER GREENS SOUP

Buttermilk Corn Bread (page 93) or Corn Muffins (page 95) are the traditional accompaniment to this soup. The greens may be all of one kind, mixed, or supplemented with kale.

SERVES 6 TO 8

  Approximately 2½ pounds collard, mustard, or turnip greens
1 medium onion
  Approximately 2 tablespoons ham or bacon fat
1 2-pound meaty hambone or 2 pounds smoked ham hocks
2 quarts water
  Dash of Tabasco
  Salt and freshly ground black pepper

Clean the greens well. Chop the leafy tops and tender parts of the stems. Soften the onion in a large soup pot in the ham or bacon fat. Add the hambone or ham hocks and the water.

Add the greens, cover the pot, and simmer the soup for about an hour. Season with Tabasco and salt and pepper if necessary. Simmer uncovered for about 30 minutes. Remove the ham from the pot and take the meat from the bones. Cut it into bite-size pieces and return it to the pot. Serve the soup hot.

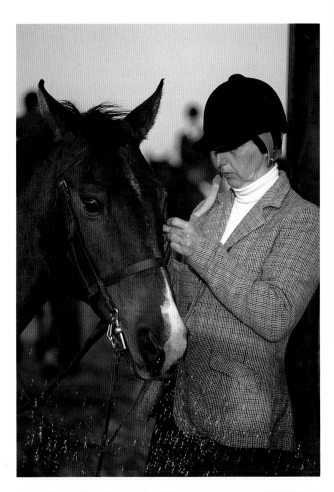

A rider makes ready for the fox chase, left, a mainland Chesapeake tradition.

In the fall, many produce farms offer pumpkin-picking, right, and hayrides for children and apple cider for everyone.

SOUPS AND CHOWDERS

WILD GOOSE AND WILD MUSHROOM SOUP

Game birds are such a treat that we throw nothing away. We save the carcasses of domestic and wild roast goose or duck in the freezer until we have two or three, then make a soup of them. Wild mushrooms, particularly chanterelles, are fairly common in wooded areas of Maryland, Virginia, and Delaware. They are also available in many specialty produce stores. For this recipe you need very woodsy-tasting mushrooms, such as chanterelles, or Italian porcini or French cèpes. If you cannot find these, substitute dried porcini or cèpes plus fresh cultivated mushrooms as indicated in the recipe.

SERVES 4 TO 6

Carcasses of 2 or 3 roasted Canada geese
Water
1 quart chicken stock
1 medium onion, peeled and cut in half
½ celery rib
½ carrot
1 or 2 sprigs of thyme, or ¼ teaspoon dried thyme leaves
¾ to 1 pound chanterelle mushrooms, or 1 ounce dried imported mushrooms plus ½ pound cultivated mushrooms
3 tablespoons unsalted butter
Salt and freshly ground black pepper

GARNISH (optional): chopped parsley

Chop the carcasses of the geese into pieces with a cleaver or heavy knife. Put them in a large soup pot. Add water to come about halfway up the bones, then add the chicken stock. Add the onion, celery, carrot, and thyme.

Simmer the broth for about 45 minutes, skimming occasionally. Taste the broth to be sure it has the rich taste of goose. Simmer a little longer if necessary. Strain the broth into a clean saucepan—you should have about 1 quart.

Meanwhile, clean the fresh mushrooms with a damp paper towel or cloth. Remove the stems and slice the mushrooms ⅛ inch thick. If you are using dried mushrooms, soak them in 1 cup of boiling water for 15 minutes or so. Strain the mushroom liquor through rinsed cheesecloth or paper towels and reserve. Rinse the softened mushrooms, discard any tough stems, and chop the mushrooms coarsely.

Melt the butter over medium-high heat and sauté the mushrooms for 5 minutes.

Add the mushrooms and any reserved mushroom liquor to the strained goose broth and simmer the soup for 5 minutes. Season with salt and freshly ground pepper to taste. Serve the soup very hot, garnished with parsley if desired.

WINTER ROOT VEGETABLE SOUP

This simple, hearty soup makes a nice change from the seafood chowders of winter. It is especially good accompanied by dark bread and a green salad.

SERVES 6

4 tablespoons unsalted butter
1 medium red onion, chopped medium fine
1 small rutabaga (about 12 ounces), peeled
2 medium red potatoes (about 1 pound), peeled or well scrubbed
2 small turnips (about 12 ounces), peeled
4 cups vegetable or light chicken stock
½ teaspoon ground allspice
¾ teaspoon freshly chopped thyme, or ¼ teaspoon dried thyme, crumbled
1 cup light cream or half-and-half
Salt and freshly ground black pepper
Pinch cayenne

GARNISH: chopped parsley

Melt the butter in a noncorrodible heavy-bottomed soup pot. Sauté the onion in the butter over medium heat for 3 or 4 minutes.

Chop the rutabaga, potatoes, and turnips into ½-inch dice. Add the rutabaga to the onions and cook, stirring, for 4 or 5 minutes. Add the potatoes and cook, stirring, for 2 to 3 minutes more. Add the turnips and cook another 2 minutes.

Add the stock to the pot along with the allspice and thyme; cover and bring to a simmer. Reduce the heat and cook for 15 to 20 minutes more, until vegetables are tender.

Puree about two-thirds of the soup in batches in a blender. Return to the pot and add the cream, salt and pepper to taste, and cayenne. Stir well, cover, and let stand over low heat for 5 minutes. Taste for seasoning. Serve the soup hot with a garnish of freshly chopped parsley.

SUCCOTASH SOUP

SERVES 4 TO 6

 4 tablespoons unsalted butter
⅔ cup fine-chopped onion
 2 cups shelled fresh lima beans
 2 cups fresh corn kernels
 2 cups light chicken or vegetable stock
 1 cup half-and-half
    Salt and freshly ground black pepper
    Generous gratings fresh nutmeg

Melt the butter in a soup pot over medium heat. Add the onions and cook for about 5 minutes, stirring occasionally. Add the lima beans and cook for another 5 minutes. Add the corn and cook for 2 minutes longer.

Add the stock, cover the pot, and cook for 8 to 10 minutes. Add the half-and-half and heat through, but do not boil.

Puree half of the soup in a blender in batches. Return to the pot and season with salt and pepper to taste and nutmeg. Cook the soup over low heat for 5 minutes. Adjust the seasoning and serve hot.

HAM AND BEAN SOUP

If you forget, or don't have time, to soak the beans overnight, cover them with 3 inches of water and bring to a boil. Simmer for 5 minutes, covered, then remove from the heat and let the beans soak in the cooking liquid for 1 to 2 hours. This is a soup best made a day before serving.

SERVES 6 TO 8

½ pound navy beans, soaked
    Ham broth, if available (optional)
 1 1- to 2-pound meaty hambone
 1 large onion, diced
 2 tablespoons olive or vegetable oil
 1 sweet green pepper, diced
 1 sweet red pepper, diced
 1 celery rib, diced
    Salt and freshly ground black pepper
    Dash of cayenne

Drain the beans and place in a soup pot. Add the ham broth if you have it or enough fresh water to cover the beans by 1 inch.

Over low heat soften the onion in the oil for about 5 minutes. Add the peppers and celery and cook for another 5 minutes. Add the vegetables to the beans and ham.

Simmer the soup for 45 to 60 minutes, until the beans are done. Remove the hambone from the soup and let it cool. Puree about half of the soup and return it to the pot. Cut the meat from the hambone and add it to the soup. Season the soup with salt, pepper, and cayenne. Serve very hot.

MELON SOUP WITH CHERRIES

This chilled soup is wonderful on those dog days of July and August when the melons are in season. It is especially delicious when served with buttered croutons sprinkled lightly with cinnamon sugar. To make a smaller amount of soup, use halves of the melons, and half of the lime juice and cherries.

SERVES 8 TO 12

 1 1½- to 2-pound ripe cantaloupe
 1 1½- to 2-pound ripe Crenshaw or honeydew
    melon
 2 teaspoons lime juice, or to taste
½ to ¾ pound ripe Bing cherries

Halve the melons and remove the seeds. Remove the pulp from the melons in large chunks and puree in batches in a blender or food processor. Transfer the puree to a bowl and stir in the lime juice.

Halve and pit the cherries. Stir them into the puree. Before serving, chill the soup for at least 1 hour, then let it sit at room temperature for about 15 minutes so that it is not icy cold when served. Stir the soup well just before serving.

SEAFOOD

Seafood has been the glory of Chesapeake cuisine for as far back as we can discover. The Algonquin Indians had already left shell middens as high as one-story houses by the time the first European settlers arrived in the seventeenth century. Stories of that time are truly astounding: shallow waters so full of crabs that bathers had to beware; fish so thick in the Potomac that white men would row into the river, iron frying pans in hand, and kill them as they leapt from the water; oyster beds so large as to be navigational hazards. Some of the early settlers were disdainful of oysters until they were able to survive a severe winter with oysters and a little cornmeal as their only food.

In the late nineteenth century, Chesapeake oysters—mainly from Maryland—were available as "Pearls of the Bay" to an eager transcontinental market recently opened by the railroads. A phenomenal 15 million bushels were harvested in 1875.

The Bay still supplies from 3 to 8 million bushels of oysters and 50 to 80 million pounds of crabs a year. As William Warner puts it regarding the soft crab catch in his excellent book *Beautiful Swimmers*: "This is not a matter of biology or habitat, but human industry. Skill, hard work, and infinite patience are required to hold crabs in 'floats' or pens until they molt, and successfully bring them live to market. People in other places don't want to do it. Practically speaking, therefore, but for the strong work ethic of Chesapeake watermen, this most delectable form of crab would never come to market."

Donald Albright and his brother-in-law Tommy Stanfield are such watermen who live and work on the Eastern Shore of Maryland. They are expert in judging when the crabs are ready to molt; they gather these "peelers" and place them in a holding pond owned by a friend just across the inlet from the Stanfield home on the Tred Avon River.

At seventy-eight, Tommy Stanfield's father still runs his own crab boat. He's up at four or five o'clock every morning during the season, judging, with the knowledge of a lifetime, the best place to set his lines. His work continues with pulling in the lines, hopeful that they're heavy with crab, culling (undersize crab must be put back in the water; dead ones likewise), and tending to the boat. Back at the dock, he sorts the crabs, baits his lines for the next day, and finishes all the tasks that will bring crab to the table. He says he has to keep crabbing because it's his life.

We're among the many who are grateful for such efforts because to our taste crab in all its forms is a true delicacy. The blue crab (*Callinectus sapidus*), tasty beautiful swimmer, is found along the Atlantic Coast in various locations, including the Gulf of Mexico, but we must follow our taste buds in judging those from the Chesapeake to be the finest—the sweetest, firmest, and least watery. In fact, of any saltwater crab we have eaten—from the Mediterranean, the Atlantic Seaboard, and the Pacific from Alaska to Baja, California—we think the Chesapeake Bay crab is the best of all.

Of course we're not alone in this ranking of the "beautiful swimmer." And further discriminations are made by those who prefer sooks (mature females) to jimmies (males), peelers (soft crabs) to steamers (hard crabs). The hierarchy can be quite precise, with preferences for crab from this or that water, this or that packer. In addition, many amateur crabbers find a goodness in the crabs they've netted themselves that goes beyond simple or gourmet tastes.

Natives of the region choose their crabs according to how they plan to cook them, the methods hallowed by both time and taste. All hard crabs can be steamed, but some people prefer males, others females. Steamed crabs are most often sold by size, and many people buy the larger males because of the favorable picking-to-eating ratio. Soft crabs are served fried, sautéed, or grilled, but cannot be steamed or made into soup. Some consider soft crab the apotheosis of crab-eating, others will not eat it. Though egg-bearing females are not harvested commercially, cooks and amateur crabbers who have tasted a version of Maryland she-crab soup still search for them to make this delicious dish.

"To pick" and all its attendant forms has a specific meaning in Chesapeake country. "Let's pick crab for dinner" in Bay lexicon means "Let's go out and eat steamed crab in a restaurant or buy steamed crab and bring it home to eat." People in inland counties in Maryland and Virginia are said by natives of the shore not to be crab pickers, though we know many devoted crab pickers in the interior.

Picking hard crab is an art, requiring both dexterity and a certain etiquette. Many people are quite happy to pound or tap or bludgeon with the little wooden mallets provided by most restaurants. But professional crab pickers and those who prize large chunks of firm, sweet meat, intact and free of shell fragments, use only a small, sharp knife and their hands to break the crab into manageable portions. The ideal knife for the connoisseur has a heavy handle that is used like a mallet to deliver one precise tap in exactly the right place, the fault line of the claw. (See page 24 for further details on how to pick crab.)

Though arguably the finest Chesapeake seafood, crab is only one of many tasty creatures found in the Bay. Oysters, with the briny, legendary Chincoteague taking pride of place, have provided the Bay with its most important seafood harvest for the past 100 years. Chesapeake oysters are still considered world class by experts—as good as, or better than, Belon, or Long Island, or Pacific varieties.

Watermen often know both crabs and oysters intimately, following the seasons to crab in summer and oyster in fall and winter. Robert Hedeen describes these men in his fascinating book *The Oyster*. "The oysterman is a breed unto himself. He knows this and is proud of his ability to challenge the forces of nature and other sources of adversity to make a living by his individual skill and physical prowess."

Jackie Russell of St. George Island, Maryland, is a young man who follows the way of the water. He's justifiably proud of his skipjack, the Chesapeake's traditional wooden oyster boat. Running his own business and boat agree with him if his sense of fun and sparkling blue eyes are any indication. The oyster he gathers, the Chesapeake oyster, is so well loved that there are hundreds of recipes for it, from baked, roasted, steamed, and fried, to oysters on the half shell and in chowders.

Shellfish in the Chesapeake are not limited to oysters and crabs, however. Clams, hard or soft, from giants weighing more than ½ pound apiece to those of silver-dollar size, are so good and so abundant that they are shipped to New England. Clams have always been in the Bay in large numbers, but they only began to be landed commercially when the New England beds showed signs of exhaustion in the 1950s. They are of excellent quality, whether the small littlenecks perfect for half-shell eating, the funny-looking soft shells, good steamed or deep-fried, or the impressively sized chowders, so flavorful in pasta sauces and soups. Lobsters, which compare favorably with catches from more northern waters, are also taken from the Atlantic beyond the Bay. There are fewer regional recipes for lobster than for crab, but it has been appreciated since the mid-nineteenth century as a special-occasion dish. Lobster and oyster pies come in savory variations of an old Chesapeake recipe that originated in England.

Local waters are also home to more than a hundred varieties of finfish, many of which are good eating. We think, as do a great many others, that the tastiest is striped bass, locally called rockfish. Commercial and sport fishing for striped bass has recently been prohibited or curtailed due to extreme population losses, but states in the region, especially Maryland, are now working on various programs to ensure the continuance of striped-bass landings—the fish taken commercially. Bluefish are another popular catch, excellent sautéed, baked, or grilled, and unsurpassed when smoked. Flounder are plentiful and are pan-fried or sometimes stuffed with crabmeat and baked. Drum, perch, and spot, usually caught by surf and sport fishermen, are pleasant-tasting fish prepared simply by frying or baking.

Fish found beyond the mouth of the Bay in the Atlantic are also making their way into the cooking of the region, with shark and sea bass particularly favored. And this partial listing does not begin to exhaust other possibilities from the Bay and nearby ocean waters, among them bay scallops, eel, herring, shad, and even shrimp.

Plentitude and quality enable local cooks to develop keen palates and wise traditions. Generally, they have followed the maxim "the simpler the preparation, the tastier the final dish." The seafood lover knows that good, solid dishes will prevail. Though the inspiration for seafood seasoning on steamed crab was truly great, other ideas, such as overly fussy crab salad with tropical fruit, or cream cheese and crab concoctions, are less mouth-watering. The right touches of fantasy inform Crab Imperials or soft crab prepared with ginger and lime. Chesapeake seafood cookery is accountable: true to its ingredients, with enough lyricism to keep it from being mundane.

The Bay has always been a primary source of an abundance of seafood, providing work for sizable populations and enjoyment to those living near and beyond its waters. Generations of cooks, watermen, scientists, and state officials have been largely untroubled by thoughts of over-fishing or pollution. The Bay had provided so much for so long that it seemed truly inexhaustible. But increasing population and land use, especially in the past three decades, have strained the processes of the great Chesapeake, the largest bay in the United States. The ecology of such large systems is complex, often slow to manifest difficulties, and is still imperfectly understood even by experts. We are very encouraged by the recent cooperation among the states whose shores or rivers touch the Bay. Their efforts to keep the Bay alive and productive are urgent and necessary to ensure that future generations will enjoy the traditions and riches of the past.

Baltimore's Inner Harbor is a lively scene, with contrasting elements of the modern and the traditional. The World Trade Center is framed by the masts; the National Aquarium is on the right.

STEAMED CRABS

Hard shelled blue crabs are quintessential Chesapeake food, riding summer's tides until a sort of steamed-crab-eating frenzy peaks in September, when crabs are plentiful and large. Festivals are held then, notably the National Hard Crab Derby and Fair in Crisfield, Maryland. Even the festival's many events and activities—crab races, a Miss Crustacean contest, marching bands, and fireworks—do not overshadow the continual steaming and eating of crabs.

Every inlet and estuary on Maryland's Eastern and Western shores, from north of Baltimore to south of Smith Island, and in Tidewater Virginia, claims its crabs are the biggest, sweetest, and best. And every cook has his or her special technique for steaming, though all agree that most important is choosing the crabs: get the real *lively crabs. A great deal of attention is paid to seafood seasoning mixes; formulas are as secret as those of perfumes, and the actual mixing is done far from inquisitive or acquisitive cooks.*

To steam the crabs, some cooks make a beer-and-water bath, some a vinegar-and-water bath, some use all three, and others, like us, hold with plain water for kettle-steaming. Many people who have homes along the water buy steamers (about the size of washing machines) to pressure-steam the crabs. Although this can result in more succulent crabs, the most important thing is to have heavy, really lively crabs. You will have to experiment with the amount of seafood seasoning; it provides a welcome piquancy that counterpoints the crabs' sweetness, but some crab eaters like it hot to a lip-numbing degree. (Most crab lovers can easily eat 6 large crabs; except at crab feasts, a little coleslaw and bread or muffins are usually the only accompaniments. The point is to eat crab. It's best to steam the crabs in batches, so that hot crabs keep coming along.)

SERVES 4 TO 8

2 dozen very lively hard shelled blue crabs
1 cup vinegar or beer for each dozen crabs (optional)
½ to 1 cup Chesapeake seafood seasoning (page 12)

Have ready a large pot with a tight-fitting lid and a rack to elevate the crabs at least 2 inches above the water. Rinse the crabs well. Put 1 quart of water in the pot, and add the vinegar or beer if desired. Put the rack in the pot. Arrange one layer of crabs on the rack and sprinkle liberally with seafood seasoning. Do not crowd the crabs; 3 or 4 for each layer is right.

Continue layering 1 dozen crabs and seafood seasoning. Cover the pot and bring the water to steaming. Steam the crabs for 20 to 30 minutes, depending on their size. The crabs will turn bright red. Serve hot. Then layer and steam the second batch.

The crabs may be cooled to room temperature and then refrigerated if you wish to serve them cold. *Never* store cooked and live crabs together. Bacteria can result from cross-contamination and may cause illness.

CRAB CAKES

Crab cakes are one of the dishes that typify Chesapeake cooking. As such, they come in many, many variations. We feel that the use of bread or cracker crumbs as filler is a misguided idea. If you have to stretch the crabmeat, make smaller cakes and serve them as appetizers. As a main course, 2 cakes are usually served per person. You may broil the cakes rather than frying them, but they will not be quite as moist or have the lovely texture that frying produces.

SERVES 4 TO 8

1 pound fresh backfin crabmeat
½ pound fresh select crabmeat
1 extra large egg
2 tablespoons mayonnaise
1 or 2 dashes Worcestershire sauce
1½ tablespoons chopped parsley
Salt and freshly ground black pepper
Oil for frying

Carefully remove the cartilage from the crab. Try to keep the pieces of crab as large as possible. Beat the egg lightly and stir in the mayonnaise, Worcestershire sauce, and parsley. Season lightly with salt and pepper. Toss the egg mixture with the crab lightly but well. Shape the mixture into 12 small crab balls or 8 large oval or round crab cakes.

Place the crab cakes on a baking sheet lined with wax paper. Cover with wax paper or plastic wrap and refrigerate for 2 hours or longer.

Fry the crab cakes in abundant oil in a deep fat fryer, wok, or deep pan at 350° for about 3 to 6 minutes, depending on size. Turn the cakes frequently while frying. The cakes should color to a medium golden brown. Drain on paper towels and serve hot.

To broil, place the crab cakes on an oiled baking sheet. Broil 6 inches from the flame in a preheated broiler, cooking for 5 minutes on each side until golden brown.

CRAB IMPERIAL

This is another justifiably famous crab dish. We like two versions: one moderately rich, the other super-rich—both delicious variations on the theme.

SERVES 6 TO 8

IMPERIAL I

1½ pounds backfin crabmeat
  2 tablespoons minced sweet green pepper
  2 tablespoons grated onion
  5 tablespoons unsalted butter
  2 tablespoons chopped parsley
  1 tablespoon dry sherry
    Dash of cayenne
½ cup heavy cream
    Salt and freshly ground black pepper
½ cup fine dry breadcrumbs

Pick the crab carefully to remove the cartilage. Keep the meat in as large pieces as possible. Soften the green pepper and onion in 2 tablespoons of the butter for a few minutes. Mix the crab, softened vegetables, parsley, sherry, cayenne, and cream. Season lightly with salt and pepper.

Just before serving the crab, preheat the oven to 450°. Fry the breadcrumbs in the remaining butter over medium-high heat for a minute or so.

Butter cleaned crab or scallop shells, or ceramic baking shells. (You may also use a 1-quart baking dish that can withstand very high heat.) Mound the crab mixture in the shells. Sprinkle the breadcrumbs over the crab. Bake for about 10 minutes, until the crab is bubbling and golden brown. Serve hot.

IMPERIAL II

1½ pounds backfin crabmeat
  3 tablespoons grated onion
¾ cup Seafood Hollandaise (page 174)
  1 tablespoon dry sherry, or 1 teaspoon more to taste
  2 tablespoons chopped parsley
    Dash of cayenne
    Salt and freshly ground black pepper
    Approximately 2 tablespoons butter for the shells or baking dishes

Preheat the oven to 450°. Remove the cartilage from the crab, keeping the pieces of crabmeat as large as possible. Toss the crab gently with the remaining ingredients, except for the butter.

Butter cleaned crab or scallop shells or ceramic baking shells. Mound the crab mixture in the shells and bake about 10 minutes, until bubbling and light golden brown. Serve hot.

SOFT SHELL CRAB WITH FETTUCCINE

Two of our favorite foods, soft crab and pasta, together— pure, simple, delicious.

SERVES 4

  2 lemons
  4 large soft crabs
  8 tablespoons unsalted butter
    Salt and freshly ground black pepper
½ cup unbleached white flour
½ pound fresh fettuccine
  2 tablespoons water
⅓ cup fresh snipped chives

GARNISH: lemon wedges; chive sprigs

Bring ample water to a boil to quick-cook the fettuccine. When the water boils, salt it generously. Squeeze 3 tablespoons of lemon juice and reserve. Cut the remaining lemon into wedges for garnish.

Dress the crabs (see page 25). Heat 4 tablespoons of the butter in a large frying pan over moderate heat. Season the crabs lightly with salt and pepper, then dust completely with a light coat of flour.

When butter sizzles, but before it colors, fry crabs belly side down for about 5 minutes. Turn and cook for about 5 minutes, until they are red and back feeler legs are crisp. When you turn the crabs, put the fettuccine in the water to cook. If fettuccine is cooked before the crabs are done, drain, remove from stove, drain, then toss with a tablespoon of butter, and keep it warm.

Remove the crabs to a serving platter and keep them warm while you make the sauce. Add the lemon juice and 2 tablespoons water to the pan in which the crabs were cooked. Place over moderately high heat and scrape up the bits from the bottom of the pan. Reduce the heat to low and add the remaining 4 tablespoons of butter in bits, stirring constantly. Adjust the seasoning, if necessary.

When the sauce is made, toss in the fettuccine and the snipped chives. Arrange the pasta and crabs on the serving platter and garnish the dish with lemon wedges and chive sprigs.

GRILLED SOFT CRAB WITH LIME GINGER SAUCE

Whether pan-frying or grilling soft crabs, it is important to dress the crabs at the last moment. See page 25 for instructions on dressing soft crabs. Other sauces good with grilled soft crabs are Tartar Sauce (page 174), or ½ cup Chili Sauce (page 65) mixed with 1 tablespoon horseradish.

SERVES 6 TO 8

 8 tablespoons unsalted butter
   Zest of 1 lime, grated
 2 tablespoons lime juice
 2 teaspoons peeled and grated fresh ginger
   Salt to taste
12 large soft crabs

Prepare a medium-hot wood or wood-charcoal fire. Have the grill rack 5 or 6 inches from the coals. Make the sauce while the fire is heating.

Melt the butter in a small pan over low heat until it clarifies (the clear golden fat will be on top and the white milky solids on the bottom of the pan). Skim off any foam and pour the clarified butter into a small pan. Stir in the lime zest, lime juice, grated ginger, and season with salt. Keep the sauce warm over a low flame while the crabs are grilling.

When the fire is medium-hot, dress the crabs. Brush them with some of the butter sauce. Grill for 5 to 7 minutes on each side. They will be cooked when they turn a rich red-brown and the back feeler legs are crisp. Transfer them to a platter and nap them with the sauce. Serve immediately.

BLUE CRAB HASH

SERVES 4 TO 6

 1 pound special grade (page 20) blue
   crabmeat
1½ pounds potatoes, boiled and peeled
 1 teaspoon Chesapeake seafood seasoning, or
   to taste
½ medium onion, about 6 ounces
 2 tablespoons vegetable oil
 2 tablespoons unsalted butter

GARNISH: lemon wedges; poached eggs (optional)

Remove bits of cartilage from the crabmeat. Cut potatoes into ½-inch cubes. Toss the crab and potatoes together with the seafood seasoning.

Chop the onion into a fine dice. Heat the oil and butter together in a large sauté pan over medium heat until the butter foams. Add the onion and cook until softened, about 5 minutes.

Add the crab and potato mixture and stir well. Adjust the seasoning, if necessary.

Cook the hash over medium heat until the bottom is browned, about 10 minutes. Invert the hash onto a warm serving platter.

Serve the hash hot, garnished with lemon wedges. If desired, top each serving with a poached egg.

BAKED OYSTERS AND HAM

SERVES 4 TO 6

 1 cup heavy cream
 1 cup milk
 1 bay leaf
 1 mace blade, or pinch ground mace
 4 onion slices, about ¼ inch thick
1½ tablespoons unsalted butter
1½ tablespoons all-purpose flour
   Salt and freshly ground black pepper
12 thin slices (about ½ pound) Virginia ham;
   prosciutto may be substituted
 2 dozen freshly shucked oysters, or 2 pints
   standard oysters, rinsed

Scald the cream and milk with the bay leaf, mace, and onion. Remove the mixture from the heat and let it steep for about 10 minutes. Remove the bay leaf, mace, and onion. Preheat the oven to 350°.

Melt the butter in a saucepan over low heat and stir in the flour. Continuing to stir, cook the roux for about 5 minutes, being careful *not* to let it brown. Add the scalded cream and milk and cook over low heat for 10 minutes, stirring to make a smooth sauce. Season with salt and pepper to taste.

Pour half of the sauce into a 1- to 1½-quart baking dish. Place 6 slices of ham on the sauce, cover with oysters, and place the remaining ham on top. Pour over the remaining sauce.

Bake for 15 minutes, until the sauce is bubbling and lightly browned. Serve hot.

Cherrystones, above, are among the Bay's several varieties of commercially important clams. Clamming, right, is a fun summertime activity for those who aren't watermen.

CLAMS WITH PASTA

This recipe may be easily doubled or tripled, and spaghetti or other long durum pasta may be used. Over the years, we have steamed clams with and without the cornmeal soaking. On the whole, it helps. Sometimes the clams have so little sand that it is not necessary, but you can't know this before steaming. Even very clean-looking clams can be quite sandy.

SERVES 2

1 dozen cherrystone clams, about 2 inches in
   diameter
2 tablespoons cornmeal
   Salt to taste
6 ounces imported linguine
1 large, ripe summer tomato, 12 ounces
2 or 3 garlic cloves
2 tablespoons fruity olive oil
2 or 3 sprigs Italian parsley (fresh cilantro)
2 or 3 sprigs oregano
   Red pepper flakes (optional)

Scrub the outside of the clams. Put them in a large container, cover them with an inch of cold water, then sprinkle with the cornmeal. Let the clams stand for 30 minutes or so. Rinse briefly before steaming.

Put the clams in a wide pan with a tight-fitting lid. Add ½ cup water and put the lid on the pan. Steam over high heat, shaking the pan occasionally, until the clams open, 5 to 10 minutes. Sometimes the clams are stubborn and take longer to open; discard any that do *not* open.

Bring abundant water to a boil for the pasta. Cool the clams on a dish until they can be handled. Remove the clams from the shells and strain the juices through a cloth- or paper-towel-lined sieve. Reserve the broth. Check to make sure the clams are not sandy; if they are, rinse them in the broth and strain it again. Chop the clams coarsely.

When the pasta water boils, add salt and stir the linguine into the water.

Dice the tomato and the garlic separately. Heat the oil over moderate heat in a frying pan. Add the garlic and cook for a minute or so. Add the tomatoes and clams. Taste the broth; if it is very salty, add just a little to the pan. If it is not too salty, add ½ cup and cook the sauce for a few minutes.

Meanwhile, chop the leaves of the parsley and oregano. Add them to the sauce after it has thickened slightly, about 5 minutes. Cook the linguine al dente and drain. Finish cooking it in the sauce for a minute or so. Serve hot with a sprinkling of red pepper flakes, if desired.

LOBSTER AND OYSTER PIE

This is an elegant, rich version of a dish popular in the nineteenth century. In simpler versions, the pie was made with oysters, bread or cracker crumbs lining the pie crust, and a little milk instead of cream. Sometimes it contained eggs and was seasoned with salt and pepper.

SERVES 6 TO 8

 1 recipe pie crust (see Cabbage Pie crust, page 148), divided into 2 pieces, one slightly larger than the other
 2 1½- to 2-pound boiled lobsters
 6 hard-cooked eggs
    Salt and freshly ground black pepper
    Powdered mace
 1 tablespoon chopped fresh tarragon leaves, or 1 teaspoon dried tarragon, crumbled
 3 tablespoons unsalted butter, cut into small pieces
20 freshly shucked oysters, or 1 pint standard oysters, rinsed
 1 cup heavy cream

Roll the larger piece of pie dough to fit a 9½-inch pie dish. Trim the edges to about ½-inch overhang. Turn the overhanging dough under to fit the rim of the dish. Cover the dough and refrigerate.

Remove the meat from the lobsters. Reserve 4 small claws with the meat intact, the coral, and tomalley. Cut the meat into bite-size pieces. Shell the eggs and cut into quarters lengthwise.

Spread the lobster meat in the prepared pie crust. Season with salt, pepper, and a sprinkling of mace. Sprinkle about one-third of the tarragon leaves over the lobster. If you are using dried tarragon, crumble about one-third of it over the lobster. Dot the meat with 1 tablespoon of the butter.

Layer the eggs over the lobster. Season with salt, pepper, and another one-third of the tarragon. Dot the eggs with 1 tablespoon of the butter.

Preheat the oven to 400°. Layer the oysters over the eggs. Season lightly with salt and pepper. Sprinkle the remaining tarragon over the oysters and dot with the remaining tablespoon of butter.

Roll the rest of the dough large enough to cover the pie. Moisten the edge of the bottom crust. Place the top crust over the pie and seal the edge by fluting or crimping. Insert the lobster claws into the top crust, creating openings about an inch from the edge of the dish and equally spaced around the pie. Bake the pie for 30 minutes.

Meanwhile, scald the cream. Sieve the coral and tomalley into the scalded cream. When the pie has baked for 30 minutes, remove it from the oven. Remove the lobster claws and reserve. Be sure the cream is still very hot; carefully pour it into the openings in the pie crust, and return the pie to the oven for 10 minutes, or until golden.

Remove the pie from the oven and let it stand for 5 minutes. Reinsert the lobster claws for presentation. Serve the pie hot, or at room temperature.

STEAMED SOFT SHELL CLAMS

The simplest way of preparing these clams, also called steamers, is one of the best. Hold the steamed clams by the necks to dip them in broth and butter. Some people peel the black skin from the necks, then eat the necks; they are tasty and chewy. Crusty bread is the best accompaniment.

SERVES 3 TO 4 AS A MAIN COURSE; 6 AS AN APPETIZER

 6 dozen soft shell clams
⅓ cup cornmeal
 1 cup cold water
    Chesapeake seafood seasoning (optional)
¼ pound unsalted butter
 2 garlic cloves, minced
 1 lemon, cut into wedges

Rinse the clams and place in a large bowl. Cover with about 1 inch cold water. Sprinkle the cornmeal on top of the water and let the clams stand for 30 to 60 minutes.

Drain the clams and rinse them again. Put them in a large pan with a tight-fitting lid and add 1 cup of water. Sprinkle with seafood seasoning if desired. Steam the clams open over high heat; the clams will open in 10 to 15 minutes. Discard any clams that do *not* open.

Meanwhile, make the garlic butter. Melt the butter over low heat with the minced garlic. Decant the clear melted butter into a dish or individual dishes for serving.

Remove the clams from the steaming broth and keep them in a warm place. Strain the broth through rinsed fine-weave cheesecloth or paper toweling and reheat it until it is very hot. Serve the broth in individual bowls, the clams in a serving dish, with a plate of lemon wedges for the table.

EVA DEVINE'S BAKED BLUEFISH

The Devine family has operated Faidley's Seafood in Baltimore for many years.

SERVES 6

    Salt and freshly ground black pepper
2 pounds bluefish fillets, skinned
3 tablespoons unsalted butter
2 medium ripe tomatoes, about 12 ounces
2 large garlic cloves
2 or 3 large basil leaves, or 1 teaspoon dried basil
    leaves
1 cup dry red wine, such as Maryland Cabernet
4 scallions, trimmed to about 4 inches of green

GARNISH (optional): 4 tablespoons Parmesan cheese, freshly grated

Salt and pepper the bluefish lightly. Rub 2 tablespoons of the butter over the fish. Use the remaining tablespoon to butter a baking dish large enough to hold the fish in one layer. Place the fillets in the baking dish. Preheat the oven to 400°.

Peel the tomatoes and remove most of the seeds. Cut the tomatoes into medium dice. Mince the garlic. Roll the basil leaves together and cut them crosswise into thin strips. Mix the tomatoes, garlic, and basil together. If you are using dried basil, crumble it and mix with the tomatoes and garlic. Spread the mixture over the fish and salt and pepper lightly.

Pour the wine over the fish. Slice the scallions on the diagonal and place them around the fish.

Bake for 15 to 20 minutes. Test for doneness with the point of a knife. The fillets should be just opaque in the center. Sprinkle the fish with the grated Parmesan, if desired, and glaze it under the broiler for 1 or 2 minutes. Serve very hot.

SMOKED BLUEFISH

Bluefish is an excellent fish for smoking. The texture is firm, satiny, and succulent, and the flavor as distinctive, in its own way, as that of salmon or tuna, though bluefish is less rich and oily. Other fish of the same size may be smoked in lieu of bluefish. Striped sea bass, sea trout, or brook trout would be good choices, requiring perhaps an hour's less smoking time because their flesh is drier. It's best to time the preparation so that the smoking can be done in a single day.

EACH SMOKED FISH WILL SERVE 2 TO 4 PEOPLE

3 or 4 bluefish (depending on the size of your
    smoker), 1 to 1½ pounds each
¾ to 1 cup kosher salt (table salt may be
    substituted but kosher salt gives a crisper
    flavor)

Use fresh, fresh fish. Gut and clean thoroughly. Rinse the cavities of all blood. Rinse the gills, heads, and mouths well.

For 3 fish, dissolve ½ cup of salt in 1 gallon of water. For 4 fish, use ¾ cup of salt. Brine the fish for 5 or 6 hours in a cool place (55° or less), or in the refrigerator if the weather is hot or humid.

Rinse the fish and place them in a dish large enough to hold them in one layer. Sprinkle the remaining salt all over the fish and cover the dish tightly with plastic wrap. Refrigerate overnight for about 8 hours.

Rinse the fish well and air-dry them in the shade away from insects for about 2 hours. A screened porch, attic, garage, or garden shed will provide the best location. Hanging the fish by their tails with clothespins on a line is an easy way to assure air circulation all around them. The fish should be dry to the touch before going into the smoker. A small fan in front of the fish is a great help, as it accomplishes this in about 2 hours.

Follow your smoker's directions for timing and the replenishment of wood chips. Generally, the fish is smoked in 8 to 10 hours, depending on the number and weight of the fish. Cool the fish to room temperature and refrigerate in airtight bags for up to 2 weeks. Or wrap the fish for the freezer. If smoked properly, they will hold well in the freezer for 6 months.

POULTRY

Who has the best chicken recipe? That question can raise the natives' hackles more than conversations about any other food except crab. The lineages of Maryland fried chicken, Delaware barbecued chicken, and Virginia fried chicken are accorded the importance of genealogies by their devotées. Family recipes are enshrined, and someone's Aunt Lally or Grandma Belle was *always* the best in a long line of fryers, barbecuers, roasters, or stewers. "Secrets" are very important, whether of ingredients or techniques. Depending on the cook, it is the dash of Tabasco, the type of fat for frying, the bath of buttermilk or milk, the coating of cornmeal or flour, or the temperature of oven or grill that guarantees succulent success. We have tested these often rival claims to see what differences they actually make and have come to the conclusion that the quality of the prime ingredient is what is most important.

We have found that some Tabasco does add a certain *je ne sais quoi* to fried chicken, but most people are just as happy with the same recipe minus the Tabasco. Lard is good for frying, but it is hard to find fresh lard, and commercially packed lard is metallic-tasting. Even chicken cooked in good-quality lard seems to be an acquired preference; many younger people who did not grow up eating lard-fried chicken prefer the flavor—or neutrality—of vegetable oils. Peanut oil is also a matter of preference and custom, but its prime advantage, a high smoking point, is moot since bone-in fried chicken cannot be cooked at high temperatures. The central issue —farmyard or supermarket chicken—is academic, since most people, even those who ate family-raised birds as children, buy their chickens in the supermarket. Here is the region's great advantage: flavorful chickens.

Confessing our own prejudices, we find cornmeal-coated chicken rather heavy and choose to coat our birds with flour. We definitely favor a bath for tenderness and juiciness, and usually opt for the flavor of buttermilk. Roasting the bird in a high oven for about one-third of the cooking time draws off a good deal of fat and gives a nice, crisp skin. Timing grill-cooked chicken, however, is a different story. The coals should be medium-hot to begin and maintain a temperature of between 300° and 350° for about a 20-minute period. Precise rules are difficult to give because of the variables, but moderate heat is essential to juicy, perfectly done barbecued chicken. To minimize the uncertainties of this process, some people partially bake the pieces and then finish them over coals, but this method does not result in the best flavor. We think it is worth the time to get to know your grill, and, above all, to keep watch while the chicken is cooking. As for charcoal, hardwood is the best, especially hickory, oak, or cherry. Mesquite charcoal is too hot for chicken, but in any case, traditionally it is not used in this area.

The Delmarva Peninsula is not only sanctuary to a great number of wild birds, but home to a thriving poultry industry as well. Named for the states—Delaware, Maryland, and Virginia—that divide its territory, the Peninsula is largely flat fertile ground, suited to agriculture. Large-scale poultry-raising has developed in the area through the efforts of a native son, Frank Perdue, who is as well known in the mid-Atlantic states for his whimsical television commercials as he is for the quality of his poultry.

Naturally there is a great variety of chicken dishes on the Peninsula. Fried chicken is a staple at church suppers and on firehouse menus. Whether fried or grilled, chicken is usually served with the bone in, but more of the newer, nontraditional recipes now call for boned chicken breasts. Chicken with Slippery Dumplings is a homey dish similar to Belgian chicken *waterzooi*. One of the best traditional dishes is chicken salad with fried oysters. The hot crunchy oysters perfectly complement the cool creamy salad. Oysters also accompany chicken (or turkey) baked with cream sauce. Pot pies enhanced with vegetables, hard-cooked eggs, or ham are still made by older cooks, those with a sure hand for pastry. Leftover chicken sometimes is made into croquettes or used as a filling for pancakes, but more commonly it is eaten as is. Most people agree with us that there is nothing finer for lunch or a picnic than fried chicken or a joint of cold roast chicken.

Modern cooks here, as in most places in the United States, have fewer choices of domestic fowl. Many cookbooks written in the last 50 years, such as *Maryland's Way*, offer recipes for guinea hen, barnyard duck, capon, squab chicken, and turkey. Today, however, most of these birds have been displaced by the Cornish game hen. In the Chesapeake, game hens are broiled or grilled, or occasionally pan-fried, and served with cooked fruit and/or wild rice, which in the early part of this century was also popular with squab, pheasant, and guinea hen. Turkey is roasted with corn bread, oyster, or chestnut stuffing. Any leftover turkey is paired with ham or peanuts and baked in cream sauce, or made into hash or croquettes. On the rare occasions when duck and domestic geese are served, they are simply roasted and accompanied by a choice of such vegetables as mushrooms, potatoes, and onions or leeks, or by baked apples.

Almost as hotly contested as recipes for chicken are "the whether and the how" of gravy. Some people never distract from the bird with the superfluity of gravy. Others don't consider a chicken dish complete without it, but then have to decide whether to serve the gravy on the side or finish the chicken in it, like a kind of fricassee. Among gravy lovers, those who "fry the chicken and make the gravy behind it" have a choice of liquid—milk, cream, or evaporated milk. The slightly tinny but undeniably rich taste of evaporated milk has quite a following among Chesapeake gravy makers. But with or without gravy, chicken is king of Chesapeake poultry, tastefully never à la king.

ROAST CHICKEN WITH *STUFFING* AND SAUERKRAUT

———

Many Baltimore families serve sauerkraut with roast poultry, usually chicken or turkey. We find it a pleasant, tart counterpoint to the richness of a roast chicken. The simple stuffing was Susan's maternal grandmother's "everyday" stuffing. Sometimes she simmered the giblets and neck with the sauerkraut until they were tender.

SERVES 6 TO 8

1 4- to 5-pound roasting chicken
   Salt and freshly ground black pepper
2 medium celery ribs, diced
1 medium onion, diced
2 tablespoons unsalted butter
4 cups fresh bread cubes, loosely packed
1 large egg
¼ cup chicken broth
2 tablespoons chopped parsley
2 pounds home-style bulk sauerkraut, or commercial sauerkraut packed in a glass jar

Rinse the chicken and pat it dry. Remove extra fat. Rub the chicken all over, inside and out, with salt and pepper.

Cook the celery and onion in the butter in a large pan until soft. Cool them a bit and toss with the bread cubes. Work in the egg and the chicken broth. Stir in the parsley and season lightly with salt and pepper. Preheat the oven to 450°. Stuff the chicken cavity loosely and truss the chicken. Put the extra stuffing in a buttered baking dish and cover tightly with a lid or foil.

Roast the chicken, breast up, on a rack in a roasting pan for 30 minutes. Cover the breast with foil and turn the bird over. Reduce the heat to 400° and roast for an additional 30 minutes. Turn the chicken and roast it another 30 minutes.

The chicken will be done in 1½ to 1¾ hours. (Bake the extra stuffing for 25 minutes.) About 5 minutes before the chicken is done, heat the sauerkraut in its juice until thoroughly hot. Remove the chicken from the oven and let it stand for about 5 minutes before carving. Serve the chicken, stuffing, and sauerkraut on a platter, or pass the sauerkraut separately.

BUTTERMILK FRIED CHICKEN

SERVES 4 TO 6

1 3½- to 4-pound frying chicken
2 cups buttermilk
1 cup milk
½ teaspoon salt
¼ teaspoon Tabasco
1 cup all-purpose flour
1 cup fine dry breadcrumbs
   Vegetable oil or lard for frying

Rinse the chicken, cut into 8 pieces, and pat it dry. Mix the buttermilk, milk, salt, and Tabasco in a large bowl. Add the chicken and soak 4 to 5 hours in a cool place, or in the refrigerator in hot or humid climates. Turn the pieces occasionally.

Drain the chicken pieces on a rack. Mix the flour and breadcrumbs together. Roll the chicken in the flour mixture, coating each piece very well. Place the pieces on a baking tray lined with wax paper and refrigerate for 30 to 60 minutes.

In a heavy frying pan large enough to hold the chicken in one layer, heat the oil or lard ½ inch deep over medium heat. Fry the chicken, turning the pieces for even browning. Reduce the heat if the chicken is browning too quickly. The breasts and wings will be done in about 20 minutes, thighs and drumsticks in about 30 minutes. Drain the chicken on absorbent paper towels. Serve hot or at room temperature. The chicken can be made a day ahead and refrigerated after it comes to room temperature.

MARYLAND FRIED CHICKEN AND CREAM GRAVY

SERVES 4 TO 6

1 3½- to 4-pound chicken
   Salt and freshly ground black pepper
   Vegetable oil for frying
   All-purpose flour for dredging
1 tablespoon unsalted butter
1 tablespoon flour
1½ cups half-and-half
1 cup milk

Cut the chicken into 8 pieces for frying. Reserve the back and wing tips for another use. Rinse the chicken and pat it dry. Rub salt and pepper into the chicken.

Use a frying pan large enough to hold the chicken in one layer. Add oil to about ½ inch depth and heat it to 360°.

Pat the flour all over the chicken. Put the thighs and drumsticks in the pan and fry, covered, for 5 minutes. Turn the pieces and add the breasts and wings. Cover and cook for 5 minutes. Uncover the pan and finish cooking the chicken, turning the pieces occasionally. The chicken should be golden brown, crisp, and cooked through in 20 to 25 minutes of total cooking time.

Remove the chicken to a serving platter and keep it warm while you make the gravy. Pour all but a tablespoon of fat from the pan. Add the butter and melt over low heat. Stir in the tablespoon of flour to make a smooth paste. Cook the mixture for 1 to 2 minutes. Mix the half-and-half and milk together, and stir the liquid into the pan. Cook until thickened, about 5 minutes. Taste for seasoning. Serve the gravy separately or pour it over the chicken.

DELMARVA BARBECUED CHICKEN

Dry-spice marinade is popular in the beach resorts of Delaware, Maryland, and Virginia. It accents the flavor of chicken and gives the skin a nice crispness.

SERVES 4 TO 6

1 3½- to 4-pound chicken
2 tablespoons vegetable oil
1 tablespoon white wine vinegar
2 teaspoons freshly ground black pepper
2 teaspoons dry mustard
2 teaspoons paprika
½ teaspoon salt

Cut the chicken into 8 pieces, reserving the backbone and wing tips for another use. Rinse the chicken and pat dry. Mix the oil and vinegar together in a small bowl. Stir in the rest of the ingredients.

Rub the marinade into the chicken pieces. Put the chicken in a dish just large enough to hold it in one layer. Marinate for 4 or 5 hours at cool room temperature, turning the chicken two or three times. If it is hot or humid, cover the chicken and marinate in the refrigerator for 6 or 8 hours. Remove from the refrigerator 30 minutes before grilling.

Prepare a medium-hot wood or wood-charcoal fire. Grill the chicken until done, about 25 minutes, turning the pieces frequently. Serve hot or at room temperature.

CHICKEN BUNDLES

Children love these. The bundles may be cooked in an oven, though their natural home is on a grill. Warn eaters not to burn their fingers when opening the bundles.

SERVES 6 TO 8

12 chicken thighs, drumsticks, or a combination
 4 medium onions
 6 potatoes, approximately ½ pound each
12 3-inch-long rosemary sprigs
12 small mild sausage links (optional)
   Salt and freshly ground black pepper
 8 tablespoons melted unsalted butter

Cut 12 3-foot-long pieces of aluminum foil. Fold them in half crosswise, dull side out. Rinse the chicken pieces and pat dry. Place one piece of chicken on each piece of foil.

Peel and halve the onions from root to stem. Cut the halves into slices about ¼ inch thick. Cut the potatoes in half lengthwise. Slice each potato half—almost, but not all the way through—into sections about ⅜ inch thick. Insert an onion slice between each potato slice.

Place each potato on the foil beside a chicken piece. Add the rosemary and the sausage, if desired. Salt and pepper everything well and drizzle the butter over the potatoes. Fold the foil to make tight packages.

Cook over a medium-hot charcoal fire for 45 minutes. Or bake in a preheated 375° oven for 45 minutes. Serve hot.

SMOKED CHICKEN BREASTS

Very tasty smoked chicken breasts can be prepared without a smoker. You need a covered barbecue grill with good controls for regulating the temperature of the fire. It is important to smoke at a low temperature for flavor and juiciness.

The ideal temperature for chicken breasts is 250°. Wood charcoal (hickory is the best, but mesquite may be used) is necessary for smoking. Briquettes leave a strong chemical taste, even more than in ordinary grilling. The breasts should weigh at least a pound each; smaller breasts dry out too much.

MAKES ENOUGH SMOKED CHICKEN FOR TWO OR THREE MEALS FOR 4 PERSONS, OR ENOUGH FOR A BUFFET FOR 10 TO 15 PEOPLE

2 cups wood chips for smoking
  Approximately 2½ pounds wood charcoal
3 or 4 whole 1- to 1¼-pounds chicken breasts
  Herb branches, especially rosemary, bay, or thyme (optional)

Soak the wood chips according to directions. Start the fire about 30 minutes before smoking the chicken.

The chicken must be partially cooked before smoking. Simmer enough lightly salted water to cover the breasts. Poach meat side down for 15 minutes. Remove from the pan immediately and drain on a rack. Drain the smoking chips.

Spread the charcoal a bit, and spread about one-quarter of the chips over the charcoal. Take the temperature of the grill with an oven thermometer if you are not used to grilling. Put the thermometer on the grill rack and put the lid on the grill. Leave it for 5 minutes, then read the temperature. It should be between 250° and 275°.

Position the chicken bone side down away from direct heat. Turn the chicken frequently. Watch closely at the beginning, every 10 minutes or so. Add small amounts of smoking chips to keep the temperature even. Once the temperature is well regulated, by using the chips and the grill's air controls, turn the chicken every 15 or 20 minutes.

For an herb smoke, add fresh herb branches in small amounts along with the smoking chips. Put them directly on the charcoal. The herbs are best added during the last hour of grilling only, unless you like a very herby flavor.

The chicken will be cooked in about 2 hours. Check for doneness using the pressure system: Press the chicken in the thickest part with your finger; it should spring back a little.

Remove the chicken from the grill and cool to room temperature. Slice thin and serve with cold cuts, or add the slices to salads, pasta dishes, or sandwiches. The chicken keeps well in the refrigerator for 7 to 10 days if well wrapped in a zip-close bag. It is so tasty that it quickly disappears from our houses.

SQUAB OR CORNISH HENS WITH APPLES AND CHESTNUT PUREE

SERVES 4

  1 pound fresh chestnuts
  1 medium onion
1½ cups milk
  1 mace blade, or a generous pinch of ground
     mace
  1 bay leaf
  1 sprig thyme, or a pinch of dried thyme leaves
     Salt and freshly ground black pepper
  2 1¼- to 1½-pound squab or Cornish hens
¾ pound apples (Stayman, Winesap, or other
     flavorful variety)
  4 or 5 large fresh sage leaves, or ¼ teaspoon
     dried sage leaves
  2 tablespoons unsalted butter
  2 tablespoons apple cider vinegar
½ cup chicken stock or water

GARNISH (optional): fresh sage leaves

With a sharp paring knife, make a slit in the tough skins of the chestnuts; peel. Slice ½ of the onion into very thin slices. Put the chestnuts and onion into a saucepan with the milk, mace, bay, and thyme. Cover and simmer for about 20 minutes.

Remove the mace blade, bay leaf, and thyme sprig, and drain the chestnuts, reserving the liquid. Rice or mash the chestnuts and onions. Stir in the cooking liquid and season lightly with salt and pepper. Keep the chestnut puree warm.

Split the squab or hens along the backbone. Press on the breastbones to flatten them. Rinse the birds well and pat dry. Salt and pepper them lightly.

Peel and core the apples and slice about ⅓ inch thick. Chop the fresh sage coarsely, or crumble the dried sage and sprinkle over the apples. Sauté the apples, sage, and ¼-inch-thick slices of the remaining onion in the butter over medium heat for about 5 minutes. The apples should be crisp-tender. Remove the apples and onion from the pan and keep them warm.

Add the vinegar to the pan, then add the birds breast-side down. Cover them with a plate and weight them with a heavy skillet or with canned goods. Remove the weights and cook for about 15 minutes over medium heat. Check to be sure the birds are browning evenly. Reposition them if necessary. Turn them over, cover, weight, and cook for

another 10 to 15 minutes, until they are done. They should be juicy, and a rich caramel brown.

Remove the birds to a serving platter, breast up, and keep them warm. Add the apples to the pan, along with the chicken stock or water. Scrape the bottom of the pan and heat the apples briefly over high heat, so that they absorb some of the pan juices. Season lightly with salt and pepper.

To serve, split each bird along the breastbone. Place on a platter and spoon any pan juices over them. Garnish with fresh sage leaves, if desired. Arrange the apples and chestnut puree on the platter.

GRILLED CORNISH HENS WITH FRESH PLUM MARINADE

SERVES 3 TO 6

  3 1¼-pound Cornish hens
  1 pound firm ripe dark plums, about 5 or 6,
     any flavorful variety
½ cup port wine
  1 tablespoon lemon juice
  1 large garlic clove, sliced
  1 teaspoon mustard powder
½ teaspoon freshly ground black pepper
¼ teaspoon salt

GARNISH: sliced dark plums

Rinse, dry, and split the hens lengthwise along the breast and backbone. Set aside.

Wash, stone, and slice 3 or 4 plums, reserving the rest for garnish. Put the sliced plums in a blender with the remaining ingredients and blend to a smooth puree. There will be bits of plum skin. Season with more lemon juice if you prefer a tart marinade.

Put the hens and the marinade in a dish large enough to hold the hens in one layer. Marinate the hens at room temperature for about 3 hours, turning them 3 or 4 times. If it is very hot or humid, marinate the hens in the refrigerator, covered, for 5 or 6 hours. Remove from the refrigerator 30 minutes before grilling.

Prepare a medium-hot wood or wood-charcoal fire. Grill the hens, bone side down first, until done, about 25 minutes. Turn and baste frequently with the marinade.

Serve the hens on a platter garnished with thinly sliced plums.

ROAST DUCK WITH SCALLIONS AND TURNIPS

Browning the duck first is not strictly necessary, but it does render quite a bit of fat and results in a crisp skin. If you don't wish to brown the duck, roast it 30 minutes, breast up, in a preheated 450° oven. Reduce the heat to 400° and turn the duck as indicated in the recipe.

SERVES 4 TO 6

- 1 5- to 6-pound fresh duck (if the duck has been frozen, it must be completely thawed)
  Salt and freshly ground black pepper
- 1 cup dry white wine
- 1½ pounds small turnips, about 1 inch in diameter, with the greens
- 3 bunches scallions
- 1 cup duck or chicken stock
- 1 tablespoon softened unsalted butter blended with 1 tablespoon all-purpose flour (optional)

Rinse the duck, pat it dry, and trim the excess fat. Prick the duck skin and fatty deposits well. Salt and pepper the duck lightly and place in a Dutch oven or other large pan. Brown it evenly on all sides over medium heat, about 25 minutes.

Preheat the oven to 400°. Transfer the duck, breast down, to a roasting pan with a rack covered with a small piece of aluminum foil to protect the skin. Pour about ¼ cup of the wine into the cavity.

Roast the duck for 30 minutes, basting with a few tablespoons of the wine. Turn and cook for 30 minutes more, basting with some more wine. Remove the duck from the oven and let it stand a few minutes.

Meanwhile, trim and clean the turnips. Select some tender turnip greens and wash them. Trim the scallions, leaving 2 or 3 inches of the green stems.

Steam the turnips just until done, about 10 minutes. Pan-steam the turnip greens in a little water for 1 or 2 minutes. Add the scallions and steam just until crisp-tender, 1 or 2 minutes. Remove the vegetables from the heat.

Remove the fat from the roasting pan, reserving 1 tablespoon. Deglaze the pan with the remaining wine and the duck or chicken stock. Reduce the sauce by about one-third and adjust the seasoning. Strain the sauce through a fine sieve into a saucepan. Stir in the butter-flour mixture if you wish to thicken the sauce. Cook about 5 minutes over low heat. Keep the sauce warm until ready to serve.

Just before serving, add the reserved duck fat to the vegetables and sauté them over high heat for 2 or 3 minutes, until lightly browned. Serve the duck on a platter garnished with the vegetables. Serve the sauce on the side.

TURKEY BREAST WITH PEANUTS

SERVES 4

- 1 pound fresh turkey breast, cut into scallops
- 2 tablespoons unsalted butter
- 2 tablespoons all-purpose flour
- ¾ cup milk
- ¾ cup chicken or turkey broth
- 1 bay leaf
- ⅛ teaspoon cayenne
  Salt and freshly ground black pepper
- 2 tablespoons lemon juice
  Dash of Tabasco and/or Worcestershire sauce (optional)
- ¼ cup shelled roasted peanuts, preferably from Virginia, chopped to resemble coarse cornmeal

Pound turkey scallops to ¼-inch thickness. Generously butter a shallow baking dish large enough to hold turkey in two layers. Preheat the oven to 425°.

Melt 2 tablespoons butter in a saucepan. Stir in the flour and cook over very low heat for about 5 minutes. Add the milk and stock all at once and stir vigorously. Add the bay leaf and the cayenne. Cook over very low heat for about 15 minutes, stirring occasionally. Season with the salt and pepper, lemon juice, and Tabasco or Worcestershire sauce, if desired. Remove the bay leaf.

Spoon ⅓ cup of the sauce into the baking dish. Place one layer of turkey over the sauce and salt and pepper it very lightly. Cover with half of the remaining sauce. Repeat the layering with the remaining ingredients. Sprinkle the chopped peanuts on top.

Bake for 10 minutes at 425°, then reduce the heat to 375° and bake another 10 minutes. The turkey should be just tender and the sauce bubbling. Turn the oven to broil and glaze the sauce under the broiler for a minute or two. Serve very hot.

—

MEAT
AND
GAME

—

Of all the food-related traditions in the Chesapeake area, none is longer or stronger than hunting. From the Indians of precolonial times to the hunters and craftsmen of today, the rituals of the search for game begin in the bright fall days of the deer season and continue through the bone-chilling winter season for geese and ducks. Young and old hone their skills and techniques, and ultimately bring to table a small portion of the great natural bounty the region offers.

Significant to goose- and duck-hunting is the rich history of the relationship between craftsmen and hunters. The Eastern Shore of Maryland is the center for decoy-making and goose-call carving. Decoys are an important, some say essential, part of bird-hunting. A decoy may be carved of wood, either full (in the round) or flat (a silhouette), or it may be a bird from the hunter's quarry that has been mounted. The mounting is done by craftsmen such as Gil Feldman, a skilled taxidermist who has been known to mount more than two hundred Canada geese in a year. This activity is very carefully regulated, as the migratory birds are federally protected, with strict bag limits. Another craftsman is Sean Mann, a world champion goose caller and call carver. He was raised on the Shore, near Easton, Maryland, where each fall a festival brings carvers and hunters from around the world who appreciate the beauty and finesse of these traditional skills.

After almost 400 years of increasing settlement, the area is still rich in game through prudent management. The threat to game in the Chesapeake region is not from the hunters, who endorse the rules that regulate the hunting seasons, but from disappearing habitats that leave the mallard ducks and other birds without nesting sites, the terrapins and muskrats without places to make their homes. But red and common deer abound and are hunted in season, and

Canada geese as well as canvasback and black ducks still migrate here in plentiful numbers.

A Canada goose, appetizingly burnished from roasting, makes a handsome presentation on the dining table. Spit-roasting used to be common for all kinds of fowl, until the kitchen fireplace with built-in spit was replaced by the wood or kerosene stove. Wild birds do not have the fat of barnyard fowl, but the Canada goose is succulent and does not require added cooking fat. The meat is very tasty but not gamy and is considered the finest eating of all Chesapeake game birds. (We do not recommend freezing most foods, but fresh-killed game birds, especially large ones such as geese and ducks, suffer little loss of taste or texture if frozen. The process actually tenderizes them most effectively, replacing the old method of hanging.) Preparations range from the elaborate—stuffing the bird with grapes and tangerines—to the simple—rubbing with butter or olive oil. Other methods include bacon-barding, adding red wine to the roasting pan, or marinating in a variety of marinades such as wine and/or wine vinegar and currant jelly or Madeira sauce. Among other game birds, quail are braised, roasted, grilled, or pan-fried, with simple sauces composed of a little stock, wine, or cream. For dove, usually only the breast is eaten, either grilled or pan-fried. Duck is roasted, or split in half lengthwise and braised, and is frequently served with pan-roasted vegetables, such as turnips, carrots, onions, or potatoes.

Venison appears in a range of dishes, depending on the cut of meat. It is often accompanied by currant jelly, though we feel the flavors are incompatible. We like the acidity of red wine much better, whether in stew, as a marinade for grilled venison, or in a sauce for roasts or fried steaks. David Lenz, a native of the Chesapeake who practices the quiet and patient bow hunt, prefers sautéed wild mushrooms with his venison. If they are not available, he sautés fresh commercial shiitakes or uses reconstituted dried shiitakes to make a sauce. He sometimes grinds the trimmings from venison to make a mid-Atlantic version of chili.

Although hunting has provided an important source of protein throughout most of the Chesapeake's history, even in earlier days those who could afford beef and lamb added these meats to their diets, and almost everyone raised pigs. Except for spiced beef, there have been few distinctive beef preparations in the region's culinary repertoire. The majority of dishes still reflect the colonial English preference for plain roasts, steaks, and stews. In the nineteenth century veal and lamb were very popular. Veal was paired with oysters or sweetbreads or roasted with herbs, while lamb was often stewed with spices, herbs, or curry powder, and combined with sweetbreads or kidneys. But the genius of the region went into pork.

In the first place, there were different versions of cured ham—brined, cold-smoked, and sugar- or salt-cured. *Maryland's Way*, a treasury of regional recipes and lore, quotes from W. B. Courtney on the making of country ham: "The most exquisite peak in culinary art is conquered when you do right by a ham, for a ham, in the very nature of the process it has undergone since last it walked on its own feet, combines in its flavor the tang of smokey autumnal woods, the maternal softness of earthy fields delivered of their crop children, the wineyness of a late sun, the intimate kiss of fertilizing rain, and the bite of fire. The making of a ham dinner, like the making of a gentleman, starts a long, long time before the event." From which we deduce a proper reverence for the porkers who gave their all, generation following generation.

Once the ham was cured there were many ways to prepare it, but often it first required long soaking and gentle simmering to be brought to perfection. As the main feature of a dinner, ham was served cold, the better to appreciate its flavor and the easier to slice as thinly as possible. Ham was also practically waste-free,

providing many slices for sandwiches, or for frying for breakfast or supper. Leftover scraps were ground to make deviled ham, ham puddings, or meat loaf. The bone seasoned greens or soups.

All parts of the hog were turned into some kind of food. Bacon was home-cured, feet were pickled, fresh chops and roasts were eaten in the butchering season, lard was rendered and the cracklings saved, sausages were made. Fresh pork in the form of spareribs or chops was barbecued, or roasted and served with greens and fried apples or applesauce. Some families layered fresh pork with sauerkraut and baked it very slowly.

Virtually all of these pork and ham dishes are still made today. Lamb, however, has somewhat declined in favor, and veal no longer is a local product and has largely been relegated to nontraditional dishes.

Judicious quantities of spices and herbs in marinades or stews or rubbed into roasts are what give our meats their characteristic Chesapeake flavor. Mace is the spice favored for veal and lamb; the preferred herbs are thyme, savory, and marjoram, with occasional use of tarragon or rosemary. Citrus zest and juice sometimes appear with lamb. Beef is cooked with ginger, cloves, and allspice when it is not served plain. Few spices or herbs are used with ham or pork, although sometimes ham is rubbed with a little ground ginger or cloves. Pork roasts or chops often are flavored with savory, and grilled or baked ribs may be basted with a complex barbecue sauce. But with meat and game, as with vegetables, it is the quality of the food itself that is most important to the Chesapeake cook.

ROAST CANADA GOOSE

We like roast goose best au naturel, *but many people serve it with currant jelly. Melt about ¼ cup of the jelly in the sauce made from the pan drippings, or serve the jelly on the side.*

SERVES 4 TO 6

1 3- to 4-pound plucked and cleaned Canada goose
1 lemon
   Salt and freshly ground black pepper
2 tablespoons unsalted butter, at room temperature (optional)

Rinse and dry the goose. Pluck any pin feathers. Cut the lemon and rub it all over the goose. Rub the bird well all over with salt and pepper. Place the whole cut lemon in the cavity.

Soak a clay roaster according to directions and put the goose in, breast up. Place in a cold oven, then turn the heat to 500°. Roast the goose for 15 minutes per pound.

Or rub the goose with the salt and pepper, then rub with the butter, and place it breast up in a shallow roasting pan or baking dish. Have the oven preheated to 450°. Roast the goose for 20 minutes, then reduce the heat to 350°. Finish cooking the goose at 15 minutes per pound.

Remove the goose to a platter and let rest for 10 minutes or so while you defat and deglaze the roasting pan to make a sauce. Add a scant cup of water to the pan and scrape it well. If you use a clay roaster, decant the juices into a saucepan. Reduce the sauce slightly over medium-high heat and season with salt and pepper.

ROASTED QUAIL WITH MADEIRA SAUCE

For a special picnic, serve the quail at room temperature with radishes and watercress, accompanied by Mrs. Ridgely's Dinner Rolls (page 45) or baguettes.

SERVES 6

12 quail
1½ cups plus 2 tablespoons Madeira
 4 shallots, sliced
 2 bay leaves, broken
 6 or 8 parsley sprigs, crushed
 1 teaspoon black peppercorns, cracked
 3 tablespoons olive oil
 1 cup chicken, duck, or game-bird stock
    Salt and freshly ground black pepper

GARNISH (optional): radishes and watercress

Place the quail in a large glass bowl with ½ cup Madeira, shallots, bay leaves, parsley, peppercorns, and olive oil. Cover and marinate in the refrigerator for 24 hours. Turn the quail 4 or 5 times.

Preheat the oven to 450°. Salt the quail lightly and pour the marinade into a roasting pan. Put the quail in the pan, breast up, and roast for 15 minutes, just until medium-rare, basting with the marinade 3 or 4 times.

Remove the quail from the roasting pan and place the pan over medium heat. Add 2 tablespoons of Madeira and scrape the pan for 1 minute or so. Add the stock and cook the sauce for 2 or 3 minutes. Strain the sauce, pressing the solids, into a small saucepan. Reduce the sauce by about one-third and season it with salt and pepper.

To serve hot, place the quail on a platter, spoon a little sauce over them, and serve with roasted shallots or leeks and new potatoes. Serve the remaining sauce in a separate dish.

For later use at a picnic, cool quail to room temperature, then refrigerate tightly wrapped.

GRILLED WILD DUCK OR DOVE BREAST WITH CRANBERRY VINEGAR

You will need whole unboned duck or dove breasts for this simple and delicious dish.

SERVES 4

3 duck or 4 dove breasts (1 to 1½ pounds)
1 cup Cranberry Vinegar (page 172)
3 large shallots, sliced
   Salt and freshly ground black pepper
4 ounces fresh cranberries
1 tablespoon sugar, or to taste

Marinate the breasts in a mixture of the vinegar and shallots for 3 or 4 hours at very cool room temperature, about 60°, or cover and refrigerate overnight. Remove the breasts and reserve the marinade.

Prepare a medium-hot wood or wood-charcoal fire. Salt and pepper the breasts lightly just before grilling. Grill them, turning frequently, from 6 to 10 minutes, depending on the size of the breasts and the heat of the fire. They should be served rare.

While the fire is being prepared, make the cranberry relish. Pour half of the marinade into a saucepan. Add the fresh cranberries and sprinkle with about a tablespoon of sugar, or to taste. Cook for about 10 minutes, until rather thick. Season lightly with salt, and more sugar if necessary. Slice grilled breasts thinly on the diagonal and serve hot on warm plates. Spoon the hot relish beside the meat.

⚜

Sean Mann, a world-champion goose caller and call carver, left, demonstrates the handiwork of Maryland's Eastern Shore cottage industry—decoy- and call-carving. Easton, Maryland, is host to the annual World Championship Goose Calling Contest.

A serene pond in Maryland, above, is a haven for Canada geese.

SPICED BEEF COOKED IN CIDER

This recipe is adapted from one in Maryland's Way.

SERVES 6 TO 8

2 ounces salt pork, cut into ¼-inch slices
2 garlic cloves, minced
2 tablespoons chopped fresh parsley
1 3- to 4-pound pot roast
2 cups apple cider
2 medium onions, chopped
½ teaspoon powdered ginger
4 whole cloves
10 allspice berries
1 bay leaf
1 teaspoon black peppercorns, cracked
  Salt and freshly ground black pepper
  Flour for dredging the roast
2 tablespoons vegetable oil
1 tablespoon unsalted butter, softened
1 tablespoon all-purpose flour

GARNISH (optional): chopped fresh parsley

Blanch salt pork for 2 minutes in boiling water. Rinse and cut again into ¼ inch wide strips. Mix the garlic and parsley together. Roll pork strips in the parsley and garlic and lard the roast by making many ½ inch deep slits with a narrow, thin-bladed knife and inserting the pork with your fingers.

Combine the cider, onions, ginger, cloves, allspice, bay leaf, and peppercorns. Marinate the roast in the mixture overnight in the refrigerator.

Remove the roast from the marinade and pat dry. Reserve the marinade. Salt and pepper the roast, then dredge it well in flour. Heat the oil in a large pot and brown the roast on all sides. Add the marinade.

Simmer for 3 hours, until the roast is very tender, turning it two or three times. Remove from the pot and keep it warm. The roast may be prepared a day ahead and refrigerated in the cooking liquid.

Degrease the liquid in the pan and press it through a strainer. There should be about 2 cups of pan juices. Mix the softened butter and the tablespoon of flour together and whisk into the strained sauce. Cook over low heat for about 5 minutes. Adjust the seasonings.

To serve, carve the roast into slices about ⅓ inch thick and arrange on a platter. Surround with baked or boiled potatoes and steamed carrots. Pour some of the sauce over the meat and serve the rest on the side. Garnish with chopped parsley if desired.

BESSON'S HAM AND BEEF LOAF

SERVES 4 TO 6

1 pound ground round steak
1 1- to 1¼-pound smoked ham, ground
2 eggs
¾ cup fresh or day-old breadcrumbs
1 cup milk
  Salt and freshly ground black pepper

Preheat the oven to 350°. Mix meats together. Beat the eggs lightly and work them into the meat. Soak breadcrumbs in the milk for about 10 minutes.

Drain the bread and mix it into the meat. Season well with pepper and lightly with salt. Pack into a buttered 9 × 5-inch loaf pan or shape into a loaf and place in a baking dish. Bake for about 1 hour and serve hot.

BAKED PORK WITH SAUERKRAUT AND APPLES

SERVES 6 TO 8

Approximately 3 pounds bulk home-style sauerkraut, or commercial sauerkraut packed in glass jars
2 large apples, Winesap or other flavorful variety
6 to 8 thin-cut pork chops, 1½ to 2 pounds
1 pound smoked ham, or small smoked link sausages
3 leeks, approximately 1 pound, or 1 medium onion
  Salt and freshly ground black pepper
1 teaspoon chopped fresh tarragon, or ½ teaspoon dried tarragon leaves, crumbled
⅓ cup chicken broth

GARNISH (optional): chopped fresh parsley

Drain the sauerkraut. Preheat the oven to 350°. Core and peel the apples and slice about ⅓ inch thick.

Trim the pork chops and ham of fat. Cut the ham into pieces about 1 inch wide by 2 inches long. If using sausages, prick them with a fork.

Trim and wash the leeks. Leave some pale green if the leeks are not too sandy. Slice crosswise about ¼ inch thick. Or cut the onion in half lengthwise, then into ¼-inch slices crosswise.

Oil a 2-quart casserole. Place half of the sauerkraut on the bottom. Arrange the chops on the sauerkraut and season them with salt and pepper. You will need *very little* salt, as the sauerkraut and ham or sausage are salty.

Arrange the ham or sausage around the chops. Layer the meats with the leeks or onion, then add the apple slices. Season lightly and sprinkle with half of the fresh tarragon or crumbled dried tarragon.

Cover with the remaining sauerkraut and sprinkle the rest of the tarragon on top. Pour the chicken stock over the dish. Cover the casserole with a lid, or tightly with foil. Bake for 1 hour. Serve very hot. Garnish with fresh chopped parsley, if you like. Boiled new potatoes are a good accompaniment.

RABBIT FRICASSEE

SERVES 4

4 ounces bacon, about 4 slices, in ½-inch dice
1 3- to 3½-pound rabbit, dressed
    Salt and freshly ground black pepper
½ cup flour for dredging
2 shallots, diced fine
2 or 3 sprigs fresh tarragon, or 1 teaspoon dried
    tarragon leaves
    Approximately ½ cup veal or chicken stock
½ cup dry sherry
12 medium mushrooms
½ cup heavy cream

GARNISH: few leaves chopped parsley and fresh
        tarragon, if available, and crumbled
        bacon

Cook the bacon over low heat in a pan large enough to hold the rabbit until it is crisp and all the fat is rendered. Drain the bacon on toweling and transfer half of the fat to a sauté pan. Reserve.

Meanwhile, rinse rabbit well and remove kidneys, connective tissue, and the flaps attached to the rib cage. Joint the rabbit. Pat dry and season lightly with salt and pepper. Dredge the pieces in flour.

Brown the rabbit in the hot fat in the large pan. Turn each piece once. The rabbit will be brown in about 10 minutes. Lower the heat and add the shallots. Cook them for 2 or 3 minutes.

Add the tarragon, stock, and sherry. Cover the pan and braise the rabbit for about an hour, turning

occasionally and adding a little stock if necessary to keep plenty of liquid in the pan.

While the rabbit is cooking, clean, trim, and quarter the mushrooms. When the rabbit is almost done, fry the mushrooms in the reserved fat until they just begin to release their juices.

Increase the heat under the rabbit and add the cream and mushrooms. Reduce the sauce by about one-third. Serve the rabbit on a warm platter, sprinkled with the parsley and tarragon and cooked bacon, crumbled. Mashed potatoes, or new potatoes in their jackets, are good with this dish.

MARINATED GRILLED
VENISON LOIN

With good wine for the marinade, and good wine to drink, the hunter and the cook will be the recipients of happy toasts. Sean Mann, a hunter and champion goose caller from Easton, Maryland, gave us this recipe, which he prepares for his family during the fall and winter holidays.

SERVES 4

1 12-ounce venison loin
4 garlic cloves, minced
½ bottle full-bodied red wine
2 teaspoons black peppercorns, cracked
    Salt to taste

GARNISH: 2 bunches watercress, cleaned and
large stems removed

Put the venison in a dish just large enough to hold it. Stir in the garlic and red wine. Cover and marinate the loin 6 to 8 hours, turning it two or three times. Marinate at very cool room temperature, about 60°. A basement or cellar is the ideal location. If this is not possible, marinate the loin in the refrigerator and remove it about 2 hours before grilling.

Prepare a medium-hot wood or wood-charcoal fire. Remove venison from the marinade and press garlic bits and cracked pepper all over it. Salt the meat lightly. Grill venison carefully; it is much leaner than beef and will be dry if overcooked. The venison will be done in 15 to 20 minutes, depending on the fire. It should be browned on the outside, but not crusty, and rare to medium-rare inside. Let the venison rest 2 or 3 minutes.

Meanwhile, garnish a serving platter with cress. Place the meat in the center of the platter and carve on a slight diagonal into ½ inch thick slices.

—

VEGETABLES
AND
SIDE DISHES

—

A 70-degree haze blankets the landscape at five o'clock on a July morning at Sharp Farms in Howard County, Maryland. Chuck Sharp and his wife, Denise Doerer, have been up for over an hour, checking the fields at the family farm and the land they rent from a neighbor. Corn and tomatoes are the priorities today. Chuck will determine which patches of corn are ripe so he can set the high-school kids to work when they arrive two hours later. Denise has been concentrating on the ripe tomatoes, picking some and selecting those to be harvested by others, so that by eight the truck will be full, ready for a run to Safeway, her first client this morning. They're practically out of Sharp's tomatoes; small wonder, when 98 percent of the time people can buy only unripe and bland-tasting tomatoes in supermarkets. Here in central Maryland, Safeway is happy to buy from the local growers because their customers insist on just-picked corn and tomatoes, green beans, and melons. Otherwise they will do all of their produce-buying at the farm stands (also clients of Chuck and Denise) that flourish along the country and suburban roads of Maryland, Delaware, and Virginia during the spring, summer, and fall.

After the large deliveries are done, the day's corn, tomatoes, melons, summer squash, green beans, and crops such as eggplant and sweet or hot peppers are picked for sale at the Sharp Farms barn. Denise and Chuck used to manage this as well, but in the past few years they have had too much else to do; a manager now maintains the high quality of their retail outlet. Chuck and Denise take telephone orders, do the accounts, and check the weather and the calendar for the planting schedules for pumpkins and other fall crops, pausing on the way to the tractor to eat a melon for breakfast.

They spend a full morning at such chores and others, phoning for an extra person to work in the fields, changing a tire on one of the wagons.

If there is time, they sit on the cool porch of their farmhouse and eat melon for lunch, with a few cookies or ice cream a friend has brought by. As Denise says, "There's no time for cooking in the summer," amplified by Chuck's assertion that "we live on melon all summer: breakfast, lunch, and dinner."

The afternoon brings more harvesting, tilling, and hay-cutting. When the weather is right, as it is most summers, with a proper balance of rain, sun, and warm temperatures, the pace on a truck farm of this size, about 175 acres, is relentless. Even with carefully staggered planting times, very often an entire patch of tomatoes needs to be picked *right now*, before a thunderstorm hits. When the weather is bad it means drought, which can wipe out the corn crop in this unirrigated region. Severe drought can mean loss of other crops as well.

The work goes on through Halloween, by which time haze and heat have been replaced by high cerulean skies and impressionistic backdrops of maple, poplar, and oak trees shimmering red, yellow, orange, green, and buff. At Sharp Farms old-fashioned hayrides carry busloads of schoolchildren out to pick pumpkins. At Larrilands, another farm open to the public, the pumpkin patch is brilliant orange and chocolate brown against a field of deep blue-green broccoli. The peaches are finished, but the apples hang like red and green ornaments. The last of summer's flowers sway in the cutting garden. The children are amused by the hay maze and the Troll Bridge with Three Billy Goats Gruff, and amazed by the seven-foot witches constructed by Deborah Hall, Larriland's resident artist. The final harvest smells of cider and crisp earthiness of just-cut mustard, turnip, and collard greens.

The dedication of the farmers here goes beyond the lovely settings they maintain; it is manifest in every fruit and vegetable produced. The farmers have an understanding with the local people who depend on them: to grow and sell the best that the area can offer.

Because the land is still relatively open, with few large urban clusters, many of the country people have their own kitchen gardens. For the townspeople and suburbanites, there are the fruit stands, so-called though they sell vegetables too, often flowers and plants, and staples such as eggs and milk. Tom and Joyce Johannes, who own Good Earth Produce in Olney, Maryland, located between the suburbs and the country, pick up produce several times a day in the season from Sharp Farms and others, so they can assure their customers that the corn was picked within the hour. This closeness to the supply is important since the Chesapeake has always depended on agriculture as well as fishing for its livelihood, rather than on industry or service businesses.

In the kitchen vegetables are treated rather simply, their natural good taste usually allowed to stand on its own. The only reason to add anything is for the sake of a little change. Vegetables are not regarded as come-lately health food or low-calorie additions to meals, nor is there an eat-your-greens-they're-good-for-you attitude. Rather, they are enjoyed and respected for their simple goodness. We've seen summer visitors surprise themselves with three or four picked-clean corncobs on their plates while the natives think nothing of polishing off five or six ears. On some tables there is a special stick of good butter just for corn, usually hollowed out in the middle with little indentations marking where the family has rolled the corn on it. Others, like us, eat corn just as it comes from its brief hot-water bath, no butter—no salt, no pepper.

Though supermarkets here have exotic vegetables and winter imports, many people eat with the seasons, shunning tomatoes and corn in winter, and preparing instead the good old-fashioned cabbage or root-vegetable dishes. In summer, vegetables are usually quickly prepared, with the exception of limas and corn, which are so perfect that it is worth heating the oven for baked succotash. On days when our

houses themselves feel as hot as an oven, our favorite supper is thick-sliced tomatoes, perhaps dressed with an herb and some olive oil, piles of sweet corn, and peach ice cream. In the fall when our taste buds quicken, we relish a plate of hot field cress and turnip or mustard greens. By December, sweet potatoes, parsnips, winter squash, beets, and rutabagas taste of the season in satisfying gratins and stews. In the warmth of the kitchen squash puff rises in the oven, and the fragrance of stewing tomatoes reminds us to check the seed catalogs, for spring and summer soon turn again.

SUCCOTASH

If you get a yen for succotash during winter, you may make it with frozen corn and limas; the cooking time will be shorter, perhaps only 10 minutes.

SERVES 6 TO 8

8 medium to large ears sweet corn,
   approximately 4 cups kernels
2 pounds fresh lima beans, approximately 3 cups
   shelled
1 cup water
1 cup half-and-half
4 tablespoons butter
1 to 2 teaspoons sugar, depending upon the
   sweetness of the corn (optional)
   Salt and freshly ground black pepper

Shuck the corn and cut the kernels from the cobs. Shell the limas and rinse and sort them.

Put the limas in a heavy, noncorrodible pot with the water. Cook covered over medium heat until the limas are barely tender, about 5 minutes. Cooking time will depend on the size and freshness of the beans. Drain and return them to the pan.

Add the corn and half-and-half to the beans and cook for about 5 minutes. Stir in the butter, and the sugar, if desired. Season with salt and pepper and cook for another 5 minutes or so. Taste for seasoning and serve hot in small bowls.

Summer Vegetable Salad is a medley of garden vegetables cooked until crisp-tender and dressed with a light vinaigrette.

SANDY SPRING CORN PUDDING

Sandy Spring is in the center of Maryland, the heart of Chesapeake sweet corn country. Ellen Hartge, who lives near Sandy Spring, has made corn pudding for many years and shared this recipe with us. She sometimes has so much corn that she bakes several batches of pudding, then packs them for the freezer—a treat for winter eating.

The corn must be at a particular stage of development to make corn pudding. It should be late harvest and have been left on the stalks for ten days to two weeks after perfect maturity for corn-on-the-cob eating. At this point, it has the requisite starch content to make pudding. This is easy to do if you are growing your own corn; otherwise you can ask your local farm stand to leave some corn for late harvest. Supermarket corn can be used with the addition of a little flour.

A corn scraper is the best tool for removing the corn. If you do not have one of these, slit the centers of each row of kernels with a small, sharp knife. After you have slit all the rows on the ear, press the tender milky corn meat down from the ear with the blunt side of a large knife.

This pudding is a fine accompaniment to simply cooked meats, especially beef and ham. It is also good as the center of a simple lunch or supper, with some buttered lima beans on the side and a salad of late-harvest tomatoes.

SERVES 4 TO 6

1 dozen ears of overripe corn (have 2 or 3 extra ears, depending on size), to make 1 quart of scraped corn
2 tablespoons unsalted butter
2 eggs
¼ cup heavy cream
3 tablespoons all-purpose flour
1 teaspoon salt
1 tablespoon sugar (optional)
  Freshly ground white pepper (optional)

Husk the corn and remove the silk. Scrape the corn with a corn scraper, or with a knife as described above, into a large bowl. The scraped corn should feel sticky with starch.

Butter a 1½-quart casserole dish with 1 tablespoon of the butter. Preheat the oven to 350°.

Beat the eggs well and stir them into the corn. Add the cream a little at a time. The amount of cream the corn will absorb depends on how starchy the corn is. Very starchy overripe corn will absorb more cream. If the corn does not feel sticky with starch, do not add the cream.

If you are using supermarket corn, sprinkle the corn and egg mixture with the flour before adding 2 tablespoons of cream. Blend the flour in well. Stir in the salt. Taste a little of the mixture; if it is very flat you may want to add sugar and white pepper to taste.

Pour the mixture into the buttered baking dish. Dot the top with the rest of the butter. Bake for 1 hour and serve hot.

ROBERT AND AUDREY'S CORN AND TOMATOES

This is a favorite summer supper dish of Robert and Audrey Belsinger, Susan's parents. Add more corn, tomatoes, and butter if you wish to serve more people, or if, as Robert says, "there's someone who likes good food."

SERVES 4

4 medium ears Silver Queen corn or sweet white corn
4 tablespoons unsalted butter
2 large tomatoes
  Salt and freshly ground black pepper
  Pinch of sugar

Cut the corn kernels from the cobs. Sauté the corn in the butter over medium-low heat for a few minutes while you prepare the tomatoes.

Core the tomatoes and chop to a fine dice. Add them to the corn. Season lightly with salt and pepper and a pinch of sugar. Cook over low heat for about 15 minutes. The tomato will be cooked into a medium-thick sauce and the corn slightly crisp-tender. Serve hot.

PARSNIPS AND POTATOES

SERVES 6

1½ pounds parsnips
  1 pound russet potatoes
  4 large garlic cloves
  2 sprigs thyme, or ¼ teaspoon dried thyme leaves
  1 cup milk
    Salt and freshly ground black pepper
  3 tablespoons unsalted butter, or ¼ cup heavy cream

Peel the parsnips and remove the woody cores. Dice them and put them in a pan and cover with cold water. Cover the pan and cook the parsnips just until done, about 15 minutes. Drain, reserving a little of the cooking liquid.

Meanwhile, peel the potatoes and dice them. Cover with cold water and cook just until done, about 15 minutes. Drain and reserve a little of the liquid.

While the parsnips and potatoes are cooking, peel the garlic cloves and put them in a small pan with the thyme and milk. Cook over low heat just until the garlic is tender, about 10 minutes. Remove the thyme and reserve the milk.

Mash parsnips, potatoes, and garlic together in a large bowl. Stir in milk and thyme. If the mixture is dry, add a little of the cooking liquid from the vegetables. Season with salt and pepper. Enrich the parsnips with butter or heavy cream, according to taste. The dish may be prepared ahead to this point.

Preheat oven to 350°. Butter a 1- or 1½-quart baking dish. Spoon parsnips and potatoes in and bake for 25 minutes, until top is lightly browned. Serve hot.

BAKED STUFFED PATTYPAN SQUASH

SERVES 8

2 pounds (approximately 8) small pattypan or summer scallop squash
2 tablespoons unsalted butter
¼ cup diced onion
1 garlic clove, crushed
½ cup diced fresh tomato
3 tablespoons fine dry breadcrumbs
2 tablespoons freshly grated Parmesan cheese
  Salt and freshly ground black pepper
½ cup dry white wine, or water

Blanch the whole squashes in lightly salted water for 12 minutes. Refresh under cold water. Remove the tops and hollow the squash, removing 1½ to 2 tablespoons of flesh and retaining the shells. Dice the flesh into small pieces. Cut thin slices from the bottoms of the squash shells if necessary to allow them to stand in a baking dish. Preheat the oven to 350°.

Melt the butter over medium heat and cook the onion for 2 or 3 minutes. Add the diced squash and garlic and cook for 1 more minute. Add tomatoes and cook for 2 or 3 minutes.

Remove the pan from the heat and stir in 2 tablespoons of the breadcrumbs, Parmesan cheese, and season with salt and pepper. Spoon the mixture into the squash shells and place them in a baking dish. Pour wine or water into the dish. Sprinkle the tops of the squash with the remaining breadcrumbs. Bake for 20 to 25 minutes, until the topping is lightly browned. Serve hot.

CABBAGE PIE

MAKES ONE 10-INCH PIE; SERVES 6 TO 8

DOUGH

2¼ cups unbleached white flour
¾ teaspoon salt
½ cup unsalted butter, chilled
4 tablespoons vegetable shortening
6 tablespoons ice water

FILLING

4 tablespoons unsalted butter
1½ pounds leeks, cleaned and trimmed
1 pound cabbage, approximately 8 cups coarsely shredded
1 extra large egg
1 cup sour cream
½ teaspoon paprika
1 teaspoon caraway seed, roasted and coarsely ground
Dash of Angostura bitters
½ teaspoon salt, or to taste
Freshly ground black pepper

To make the dough, put the flour and salt in a food processor and pulse to mix. Add the butter and shortening to the processor and pulse until the mixture is a very coarse meal. If mixing by hand, toss the flour and salt in a bowl. Then cut the butter and shortening into the flour with a pastry blender until the mixture is a coarse meal.

Add 4 tablespoons of the water and pulse or mix with a fork. Add the remaining water while the processor is running and mix just until the dough starts to gather into a ball, or mix the dough by hand in the bowl just until it comes together.

Turn the dough onto a work surface and gather it into a ball, using the ball to gather up any loose bits of dough. Pinch a large walnut-size piece of dough from the ball. Using the heel of your hand, push the dough away, flattening it across the work surface. Repeat this process with all the dough. When all the dough has been spread, gather it together and repeat the process.

Divide the dough into two parts and flatten them into disks about 1 inch thick. Put in plastic wrap and refrigerate for at least 30 minutes. The dough can also be prepared ahead of time and kept refrigerated.

While the dough is chilling, prepare the filling ingredients. Melt 4 tablespoons butter in a large skil-let. Halve the leeks lengthwise and slice them about ¼ inch thick. Sauté the leeks in the butter for a few minutes. Add the cabbage, a handful at a time, stirring well after each addition. Cover the pan, reduce the heat to medium-low, and cook for about 10 minutes.

Remove the pan from the heat. Beat the egg into the sour cream. Add the paprika, caraway, bitters, and salt and pepper; blend well. Stir the sour cream mixture into the cabbage and toss to coat the vegetables evenly.

Preheat the oven to 375°. If the dough is very cold, let it stand for about 15 minutes before rolling it out. Roll one portion of dough on a lightly floured board or pastry cloth to about ⅛ inch thick. Place the dough in a 10-inch pie plate. Roll the other portion of dough to ⅛-inch thickness. Fill the pie shell with the cabbage filling. Cover with the remaining portion of dough, and trim and fold the edges under. Crimp or press the edge of the crust into a decorative pattern. Prick the top crust a few times with a fork.

Bake the pie for about 30 minutes, or until the crust is golden brown. Let the pie stand for about 5 minutes before cutting. Serve hot.

SUMMER VEGETABLE STEW

SERVES 6 TO 8

1 medium onion, quartered and sliced
3 tablespoons olive or vegetable oil
1 pound new potatoes, sliced thin
1 sweet green pepper, quartered and cut into strips
1 medium zucchini, sliced
1 medium yellow summer squash, sliced
2 medium tomatoes, diced
3 garlic cloves, sliced thin
Salt and freshly ground black pepper

Sauté the onion in the oil over medium heat for 3 to 4 minutes. Add the potatoes, stir well, cover, and cook for 7 or 8 minutes. Add the green pepper, stir, cover, and cook for 5 minutes. Add the squashes, stir, cover, and cook for 5 minutes.

Add the tomatoes and garlic and simmer, uncovered, over low heat for about 15 minutes. Stir occasionally and season with salt and pepper. Serve hot.

EASTERN SHORE FRIED TOMATOES

Some like green fried tomatoes; others like red. We prefer to use tomatoes that are almost ripe, still firm, and not overly juicy.

SERVES 4 TO 6

4 large tomatoes
   Approximately ½ cup unbleached white flour
¼ cup vegetable oil
   Salt and freshly ground black pepper
1 teaspoon sugar (optional)

Cut the tomatoes into slices about ⅓ inch thick. Dredge the slices in the flour. Heat about 1 tablespoon of the oil in a large skillet. When the oil is hot but not smoking, add the tomato slices in one layer. Fry on each side for about 4 minutes, or until golden brown.

Remove the tomatoes from the pan and drain on a warm plate lined with a paper towel. Continue until all the tomatoes have been fried, adding a little oil to the pan as needed. Place the fried tomatoes on a warm serving platter and season with salt and pepper, and sugar, if desired. Serve immediately.

FRESH TOMATO PIE

This is a wonderful summer brunch dish or accompaniment to grilled food. The pie shell may be baked the day before and stored at room temperature, well wrapped in foil.

ONE 9-INCH-SQUARE TART PAN; SERVES 4 TO 6

10 tablespoons unsalted butter, well chilled
 1 cup unbleached white flour
¼ cup stone-ground cornmeal
½ teaspoon salt
 2 or 3 tablespoons ice water
 2 or 3 large, firm, ripe tomatoes
½ pound sharp cheddar cheese, freshly grated
   Salt and freshly ground black pepper

Cut the butter into bits. Mix the flour, cornmeal, and salt. Cut in the butter with a pastry cutter, or in a food processor with the steel blade, to make a coarse meal. Add just enough water to bind the dough, and gather the pastry to form a flattened round, about ¾ inch thick. Cover the round with plastic wrap and chill at least 30 minutes.

Preheat the oven to 375°. Press the dough into a 9-inch-square tart pan with a removable bottom. Cover and chill at least another 30 minutes. Bake for 25 minutes, until golden brown.

While the shell is baking, cut the tomatoes into slices at least ½ inch thick. Remove the shell from the oven and spread the grated cheese over the bottom. Arrange the tomato slices on the cheese and season with salt and pepper. Bake for 5 to 10 minutes more, until the cheese is melted. Let the tart stand for 5 minutes before cutting.

GERMAN-STYLE FRIED NOODLES

This recipe was passed down from Susan's German great-grandmother. She usually served the noodles with roast beef and gravy, cooked spinach, and a salad. The noodles are good with gravy, though a bit heavy; we like them with stewed tomatoes.

SERVES 6

8 tablespoons unsalted butter, softened
1 medium yellow onion, quartered and cut
   lengthwise into thin slices
1 pound broad egg noodles, cooked al dente and
   drained
   Salt and freshly ground black pepper

Melt half the butter in a large skillet. Add the onion pieces and noodles all at once. Cook over medium heat, turning the noodles so that they don't stick. They absorb butter as they brown, so add more butter if necessary.

Cook for 35 to 45 minutes, until golden brown. Season with salt and freshly ground pepper to taste. Serve hot.

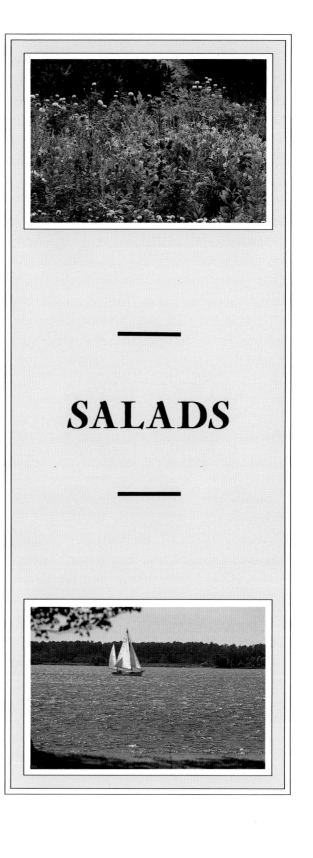

SALADS

Historic St. Mary's City in southern Maryland is a beautiful setting in which to discover the day-to-day life of the early colonial settlers. Much of their time and energy were spent in the sowing and reaping of crops and the preparation and partaking of food. Such activities as fish-smoking, corn-planting, hog-butchering, and pie-baking at an open hearth are enthusiastically reenacted by the staff of St. Mary's City. Most fascinating of all, we think, is the kitchen garden of the reconstructed late-sixteenth-century home. Here you can find the herbs and salad greens so beloved by the early English, continuing testament to the great herbalists Gerard, Parkinson, Coles, and Evelyn. Their traditions were imported into the new world with the conviction that herb simples as remedies and prescriptions for wholesome eating would ensure survival and with the hope that old-world plants would thrive. And they did flourish, providing the colonials with at the very least a richness of "sallets" (salads) beside which our supermarket selection of usually three or four kinds of lettuce seems impoverished.

With purslane, dandelion greens, salad burnet, corn salad, sorrel, the tender leaves and flowers of marjoram, thyme, and sage, and nasturtium, violet, and rose petals, salads were cheerful and interesting additions to meals. Even the scarcity of vinegar and oil could not diminish a salad with such ingredients. Salads were so much a part of the householder's life that recipes were not written for them, or indeed for vegetables in general. Cookbooks preserved only the unusual, the difficult, or basic techniques. A considerable body of knowledge about food was commonly held in peoples' minds and verbally shared with others. Some undoubtedly mastered the assembly of salads with herbs and plants grown specifically for their nutritional or medicinal value. Others gathered and were nourished by whatever grew wild in season.

Cooked salads, called pot salads or hot salads, were another traditional English dish that took root in the Chesapeake area. The tender shoots of pokeweed were used, requiring some knowledge by the gatherer since pokeweed roots are poisonous. Dandelions and field cress also were common pot herbs and are still used by some cooks. (Young field cress is tasty in raw salads too.) Hot salads today are made with mustard, turnip, or collard greens, usually dressed with apple cider vinegar and sometimes seasoned with a little ham fat or even lard, though the use of oil has become more prevalent. The greens are thoroughly cooked for these dishes; their bitterness abates and they take on a mellowness when they are simmered for 20 or 30 minutes. Old recipes call for cooking them up to an hour, but we think a shorter cooking time results in the best flavor. When they are cut and cooked in the water that clings to them, the greens will absorb the pan juices, leaving only a tablespoon or two in the pot. If there happens to be more, we drink it as an excellent cocktail.

A particular fondness for ham, chicken, and crab salads is evident here. Mayonnaise is the preferred dressing for such cold-meat and seafood salads, and is used with lettuce, tomato, and vegetable salads as well. Only a generation ago, sugar, salt, pepper, and mayonnaise were by far the most popular salad-dressing condiments. Now oil, vinegar, and other ingredients are used. Crab salad may be as simple as the best backfin crabmeat sprinkled lightly with lemon juice and perhaps capers, and served on the crispest lettuce. Or the crab may be tossed with a little homemade tomato relish or sauce, with or without the addition of mayonnaise, and garnished with sweet, icy Eastern Shore melon. Chicken salad may be dressed with sour cream or plain yogurt, and may include herbs, celery, onions, sweet peppers, or cucumbers. Ham salad is still made with mayonnaise, and with onions, celery, and often pickles, either sweet or sour.

These salads, along with potato salads and coleslaw, are the mainstays of summer meals. Formulas for concocting potato salads and coleslaw are rather loose, depending on the cook's whim and what is on hand in the crisper as well as in recipes. Potato salad may come with mayonnaise, or vinaigrette, or both, and sometimes includes a variety of vegetables, with celery and onions basic, and even bacon or leftover roast beef. We have never seen a coleslaw with meat, but have eaten one with Bay shrimp. Vegetables are also mixed in, carrots and sweet red and green peppers being the most popular.

When the days are long and hot and humid, a craving for salad sets in. Sometimes even crab does not appeal, but visions of coleslaw or garden greens shimmer like an oasis. Making a salad in the Chesapeake's summer heat, we sense the almost palpable presence of the colonials. We imagine that they instruct our composition and arouse our curiosity about edible weeds. A sensory kinship comes from the plants themselves —our walk to the garden with basket and knife, the cool water splashing over our hands as we rinse the greens. Such a salad is as refreshing as a drink of cold well water.

FLOWER GARDEN SALAD

The amounts of greens, herbs, and flowers suggested are approximate; adjust them to suit your taste and for what is in season. Do not use too many varieties or the salad will not be vibrant and clean-tasting. Flower and herb blossoms should be from unsprayed gardens.

SERVES 6 TO 8

3 quarts tender, sweet mixed greens: corn salad, spinach, oak leaf, red leaf, or other loose leaf lettuces
½ cup mixed herb blossoms: chive, summer savory, thyme, rosemary, mint, sage, lavender, borage, bergamot, coriander, or chervil
⅓ cup fruity olive oil
1 or 2 tablespoons white wine vinegar or lemon juice
Salt and freshly ground black pepper
1 cup mixed or single flower blossoms: nasturtiums, marigolds, roses, violas, day lilies, daisies, carnations, calendulas, honeysuckle, or scented geraniums

Toss the greens with the herb blossoms. Mix the olive oil, vinegar or lemon juice together, and season with salt and pepper. Toss with the greens and herb blossoms. The salad should be lightly but completely coated. Arrange the salad informally on a platter and scatter the flower blossoms over it.

SPINACH SALAD WITH BLUE CHEESE AND PECANS

Taken together, the ingredients give a perfect bite to this salad. The spinach and lettuce are wholesome and green-tasting, the cucumber is crisp and refreshing, the blue cheese is tangy yet creamy, and the nuts are crunchy and slightly sweet. Any nice, tender baby lettuce will do here, and sometimes we even add a little watercress or sorrel. Homemade garlic croutons or crusty French bread make good accompaniments.

SERVES 4 TO 6

½ pound fresh spinach leaves, washed and trimmed
1 small head butter, Boston, or black-seeded Simpson lettuce
1 small cucumber, peeled, halved lengthwise, and cut crosswise into ⅛-inch slices
4 ounces blue cheese, crumbled
¾ cup pecans, lightly toasted and broken into large pieces
½ cup olive oil
2 to 3 tablespoons red or white wine vinegar
½ teaspoon Dijon-style mustard
1 garlic clove, crushed
Salt and freshly ground black pepper

Gently tear the spinach and lettuce leaves into large pieces and arrange in a salad bowl or on a platter. Arrange the cucumber over the greens and crumble the cheese over the salad. Sprinkle the pecans on top.

Combine the oil, vinegar, mustard, and garlic. Blend the dressing well and season it with salt and pepper. Just before serving the salad, drizzle a little vinaigrette over it, and grind a bit of fresh pepper over the top. Serve immediately, passing the remaining vinaigrette.

EASTERN SHORE HEAD LETTUCE SALAD

SERVES 4

1 firm head lettuce, such as iceberg, about 1½ pounds
2 hard-cooked eggs
½ cup Homemade Mayonnaise (page 174)
1 tablespoon white wine vinegar, or to taste
   Salt and freshly ground black pepper
   Pinch of sugar (optional)

GARNISH: 1 red ripe tomato, cut into wedges or slices

Wash and core the lettuce. Slice the lettuce into rounds about ¾ inch thick. Use center slices; reserve the ends for another use. Shell and quarter the eggs. Mix the mayonnaise and vinegar. Season the dressing lightly with salt and pepper, and a bit of sugar, if desired.

Arrange the lettuce, eggs, and tomatoes on a platter or salad plates. Salt and pepper lightly. Divide the dressing over the lettuce and serve.

A young visitor, below, is ready to lend a hand filling the fruit baskets.

CRAB SALAD WITH MELON

SERVES 4 TO 6

1 pound backfin crabmeat
¼ cup sour cream
¼ cup mayonnaise
2 or 3 tablespoons Chili Sauce (page 65)
   Salt and freshly ground black pepper
   Few drops of lemon juice
½ small cantaloupe
½ small honeydew
   Lettuce leaves

Pick the crab carefully to remove cartilage. Keep the crab in large pieces. Mix the sour cream, mayonnaise, and chili sauce and toss lightly with the crab. Season with salt, pepper, and lemon juice. The salad may be chilled for a few hours before serving.

Cut the melons into thin slices and remove the rind. The melon may be prepared ahead and chilled; drain the juice before assembling salad.

Adjust the seasoning of the salad. Line salad plates with the lettuce. Mound the crab in the center of the plates and arrange the melons around the edges.

Many small-town homes on the Delmarva Peninsula, right, are graced by picket fences—and in summer, by flowers.

POTATO, GREEN BEAN, AND BACON SALAD

——

SERVES 6 TO 8

2 pounds small white or red potatoes
1 pound green beans
½ pound bacon, or 8 slices
⅓ cup salad oil
1 shallot, diced fine
1 or 2 garlic cloves, minced
4 to 5 tablespoons red wine vinegar
½ teaspoon salt
  Freshly ground black pepper

GARNISHES (optional): garden lettuces
              3 or 4 hard-cooked eggs

Boil or steam the potatoes in their jackets just until done. Steam or blanch the green beans until crisp-tender. Cook the bacon crisp and save the rendered fat. Drain the bacon on paper towels.

Mix the rendered fat with enough salad oil to make ½ cup. Add the shallot, garlic, and vinegar and mix well. Season well with salt and pepper.

Line a serving platter with lettuce, if you wish. Slice the potatoes (peeled, if you prefer) according to their shape: rounds, wedges, or lengthwise slices. Arrange the potatoes, bacon slices, and beans on the lettuce or only on the platter. Arrange the quartered or sliced eggs on the salad, if desired. To serve, drizzle the dressing over the salad.

——

CHICKEN CUCUMBER SALAD

——

SERVES 4 TO 6

1 medium carrot
1½ medium celery ribs
1 medium sweet onion
1 3- to 3½-pound chicken
1 or 2 parsley sprigs
1 or 2 tarragon sprigs (optional)
1 large cucumber
  Salt and freshly ground black pepper
½ cup Homemade Mayonnaise (page 174)
1 tablespoon chopped fresh parsley
2 teaspoons chopped fresh tarragon
  Lemon juice to taste

Coarsely chop the carrot, one-half of a celery rib, and one-half of the onion. Place the chicken in a large pot with water to cover. Add the celery and onion, the parsley, tarragon sprigs if using, and a little salt. Cover and poach the chicken until it is cooked through, but not overcooked, about 50 minutes. Turn the chicken twice during the poaching. Drain and cool. The chicken may be cooked a day ahead, cooled to room temperature, and stored tightly wrapped in the refrigerator.

Remove the chicken from the bones and discard the skin. Tear or cut the meat into bite-size pieces.

Peel and seed the cucumber and cut into slices about ¼ inch thick. Dice the remaining celery rib and ½ onion into ¼-inch pieces.

Toss the chicken and vegetables together and season lightly with salt and pepper. Add the mayonnaise and herbs and a little lemon juice. Toss the salad. Cover and refrigerate for at least an hour.

Let the salad stand at room temperature for 10 to 15 minutes before serving; adjust the seasoning.

——

CUCUMBER SLICES WITH SOUR CREAM AND ONIONS

——

Almost every family we know prepares a recipe similar to this one—it is just plain simple and delicious. It is best made 30 to 60 minutes before serving. This version is from our friend Deborah Hall, who learned it from her grandmother.

SERVES 4

3 large cucumbers, peeled and cut into fairly
  thin slices
3 tablespoons grated onion
½ cup sour cream
2 teaspoons sugar
1½ tablespoons cider vinegar or lemon juice
  Salt and freshly ground black pepper

Put the cucumber slices in a bowl. Combine remaining ingredients in a small bowl and blend well. Pour the sauce over the cucumbers and toss well. The cucumbers give off quite a bit of juice while marinating, so more sour cream may need to be added before serving the salad.

Cover the bowl with plastic wrap and refrigerate. Remove about 10 minutes before serving, so that the salad is still well chilled, but not ice cold. Drain excess liquid. Taste for seasoning and sour cream.

HOT GREENS SALAD

——

Choose two or three of your favorite greens for this dish. Older greens have heavy stems; you will need to buy the larger amount in this case.

SERVES 6 TO 8

2 to 3 pounds mixed greens: collard, mustard, turnip, kale, beet greens, or field cress
¼ pound bacon, or 4 slices
2 or 3 garlic cloves, minced
2 or 3 tablespoons cider vinegar
  Dash of cayenne or Tabasco
  Salt to taste

Remove the large stems from the greens. Rinse the greens well and put in a large noncorrodible pan with a tight-fitting lid. Cover and cook over low heat for about 20 minutes. Check to be sure that the greens are not sticking to the pan; add a little water if necessary.

Meanwhile, fry the bacon until it is crisp. Drain on paper toweling and reserve the fat.

Add the garlic, vinegar, and 2 or 3 tablespoons of the reserved bacon fat to the greens. Season with cayenne or Tabasco and salt, and cook for another few minutes.

Transfer the greens to a warm serving dish and crumble the bacon over them. Serve immediately.

SPRING SALAD OF WATERCRESS AND STRAWBERRIES

——

Two of our favorite spring foods are joined here to make a titillating salad. If hazelnut oil is not available, use olive oil instead.

SERVES 6

1 large bunch watercress
1 pint ripe strawberries
¼ cup fruity olive oil
2 tablespoons hazelnut or olive oil
1 to 1½ tablespoons balsamic or raspberry vinegar
  Salt and freshly ground black pepper

Wash the cress and remove the large stems. Rinse the berries, remove the green tops and cores, and cut into ¼-inch slices.

Combine the oils and vinegar with a fork in a small bowl. Lightly season with salt and pepper.

Arrange the cress and strawberries on six chilled salad plates. Drizzle a little vinaigrette over each salad, then garnish with a bit of freshly ground pepper. Serve immediately.

SUMMER VEGETABLE SALAD

——

SERVES 4 TO 6

2 or 3 zucchini, about 12 ounces
2 or 3 yellow squash, about 12 ounces
2 medium carrots
½ sweet-tasting onion, cut from stem to root
1½ tablespoons chopped fresh basil
1 teaspoon chopped fresh marjoram
1 tablespoon lemon juice
⅓ cup olive oil
2 teaspoons Dijon-style mustard
  Salt and freshly ground black pepper

GARNISH: 10 or 12 cherry tomatoes

If the squash are small, cut into ¼-inch rounds. If they are large, cut lengthwise, seed them, and cut into batons about ¼ inch thick and 3 inches long. Cut the carrots about ¼ inch thick, in rounds or on the diagonal.

Pan-steam or blanch the squash and carrots separately until crisp-tender. Refresh under cold water. Drain well and pat dry.

Mix the herbs, lemon juice, oil, and mustard. Season well with salt and pepper. Toss with the cut vegetables. Garnish with halved or whole cherry tomatoes and serve.

DESSERTS

Desserts are as close as many Americans come to preparing everyday food in a ritualistic way.

In common with most dedicated cooks, both of us have many memories of sweets-loving grandmothers and ice cream-expert grandfathers. Whether we were baking cakes and cookies or cutting fruit, the smallest tasks were rituals that were taken seriously. Should we finish with the silver dragées (wonderful magical words)—or the chocolate sprinkles that tasted so good on the buttercream icing—or both for a gay fillip so pleasing to the six-year-old aesthetic? How many chocolate chips was a cookie maker allowed to eat before stirring them into the dough? And then how much dough could we eat before baking the cookies? How small should the pieces of apricots or peaches be cut to add to homemade ice cream?

Ceremonies like these still apply to the rural or suburban dessert maker, who doesn't have access to fine urban bakeries. In the Chesapeake area there is such a collective sweet tooth that cooks become expert in one specialty or several. Cakes large and small, puddings and pies, crisps and ice creams—all are homemade sweets that can be found here on cake stands, in cookie jars, cooling on porches, or in freezers.

Susan Belsinger's maternal grandmother, Ella Bauer, always set a table on Christmas morning with her specialties, from sugar cookies—iced and plain—and pound cake with chocolate frosting to other cookies and cakes as took her fancy, perhaps spice or walnut, or fruitcake. She garnished the table with fruit and wine. Alma Belsinger, Susan's paternal grandmother, was a coconut-cake specialist, for which she would buy freshly grated coconut at a Baltimore city market. And Susan's maternal grandfather, Bill Bauer, was an adventurous ice cream maker, reaching beyond the usual favorites of vanilla, chocolate, and peach to create his rum bisque with raisins.

There is still a seasonal rhythm to dessert-making. Fresh fruit pies are baked spring through fall according to the availability of strawberries, rhubarb, cherries, peaches, and apples. Winter is the time for pumpkin or apple pies, and mince pies made with or without meat. The pie menu is varied throughout the year with tarts, crisps, or cobblers and by combining berries and other fruits. Shortcakes are the spring and early summer desserts, whether the traditional strawberry or mixed fruit such as raspberry and peach.

Bakery treats are usually more elaborate or time-consuming to make. One Chesapeake classic is the Lady Baltimore cake, still found on bakery shelves although it is almost too rich to contemplate, much less to eat. This confection is a yellow cake filled with walnuts, raisins, and figs, and spread and iced with boiled white icing. Fillings and orthodontia must be firmly in place before you tuck into a piece of this! Kossuth cakes—named for a nineteenth-century Hungarian general—are also professional bakers' specialties: individual sponge cakes filled with whipped cream and topped with chocolate or strawberry icing.

Homemade desserts, however, are considered the best; rare is the cook, no matter how busy he or she may be, who will not turn out a family or favorite recipe for a special occasion. When we make a sweet, from a simple crisp to an elaborate layer cake, we feel that the rites of our childhood are being reconsecrated.

MEMA ELLA'S POUND CAKE

Susan remembers her grandmother making this cake for every birthday and every family holiday. No question that the most popular frosting was chocolate, but the cake is quite good without frosting, served plain, or with fruit and ice cream.

MAKES ONE 10-INCH TUBE CAKE

1 cup unsalted butter, softened
½ cup margarine, softened
3 cups sugar
5 large eggs
3 cups all-purpose flour
¼ teaspoon baking powder
½ teaspoon salt
1 cup milk
2 teaspoons pure vanilla extract
  Simple Chocolate Frosting (optional)

Butter a 10-inch tube pan. Combine the butter and margarine and cream well. Add the sugar gradually, beating well after each addition. Add the eggs, one at a time, and mix well after each addition.

Mix the dry ingredients together and sift. Add to the egg mixture in three batches, alternating with the milk. Blend well and stir in the vanilla.

Pour the batter into the prepared pan and place in a cold oven. Turn the oven to 300° and bake the cake for 1½ hours, until a tester comes out clean. Cool the cake for 20 minutes in the pan, then turn it onto a baking rack and cool to room temperature.

Frost with Simple Chocolate Frosting, if desired.

SIMPLE CHOCOLATE FROSTING

MAKES APPROXIMATELY 1¼ CUPS, ENOUGH TO FROST A POUND CAKE OR A ONE-LAYER CAKE

4 tablespoons unsalted butter, softened
2 cups confectioners' sugar
¼ cup unsweetened cocoa
2 tablespoons half-and-half
¾ teaspoon pure vanilla extract

Cream the butter in a small bowl. Mix the sugar with the cocoa and add to the butter alternately with the half-and-half and vanilla. Beat by hand until creamy and frost the top and sides of the cake.

PEAR CRISP

Sometimes we replace two of the pears with two tart apples.

SERVES 6 TO 8

5 medium pears, Bosc, Bartlett, or d'Anjou
1½ to 2 tablespoons lemon juice
⅔ cup unbleached white flour

⅔ cup packed light brown sugar
½ cup unsalted butter, cut into 8 pieces
2 or 3 pinches of salt
2 or 3 pinches of allspice
  Generous grating of nutmeg

Preheat the oven to 350°. Generously butter a 1½- to 2-quart baking dish. Pare, core, and slice the fruit into the dish. Sprinkle the lemon juice over the fruit.

Work the remaining ingredients together with a pastry blender just until blended; do not overmix.

Spread the flour mixture over the fruit. Bake for 35 to 45 minutes, until the fruit is tender and the top is golden brown. Serve warm or at room temperature.

PEACH COBBLER

SERVES 6 TO 8

6 cups sliced ripe peaches, approximately 2½ pounds
½ cup plus 1½ tablespoons sugar
¼ to ⅓ cup light brown sugar, tightly packed
1 tablespoon fresh lemon juice
2 tablespoons cornstarch
⅛ teaspoon freshly grated nutmeg
1⅔ cups unbleached white flour
2 teaspoons baking powder
½ teaspoon salt
5 tablespoons unsalted butter, cold
1 cup milk

GARNISH (optional): vanilla ice cream

Preheat the oven to 425°. Butter a 1½- to 2-quart baking dish.

Toss the peaches with ½ cup sugar, and ¼ to ⅓ cup brown sugar, depending on the sweetness of the peaches. Add the lemon juice, cornstarch, and nutmeg and stir well. Reserve.

Mix the flour with the remaining sugar, baking powder, and salt. Cut the butter into the flour in pea-size bits. Add the milk and combine just until blended. Do not overmix.

Transfer the peaches to the baking dish and drop large spoonfuls of the dough over the peaches. Bake for 25 minutes, or until the peaches are bubbling and the top is golden brown. Serve warm or at room temperature, with vanilla ice cream, if desired.

PEACH AND BLUEBERRY PIE

MAKES ONE 9½- OR 10-INCH PIE

DOUBLE PIE CRUST

2 cups unbleached white flour
½ teaspoon salt
1 tablespoon sugar
½ cup cold unsalted butter
4 tablespoons vegetable shortening
4 to 6 tablespoons ice water

FILLING

2½ pounds firm, ripe peaches, peeled
1 pint blueberries, rinsed and sorted
⅓ to ½ cup sugar (use larger quantity if peaches are tart)
3 tablespoons all-purpose flour
Freshly grated nutmeg
1 tablespoon milk and 2 teaspoons sugar (glaze)

To make the crust, mix the flour, salt, and sugar. Cut in the butter and shortening with a pastry cutter or in a food processor. Add the water, stirring with a fork or pulsing in the processor, a tablespoon at a time, until the dough just holds together. Pat the dough into two rounds, one a bit larger than the other, each about ½ inch thick. Cover the dough with plastic wrap and chill for at least 30 minutes. The dough may also be frozen for up to a month. Remove from the freezer and let thaw in the refrigerator for 6 to 8 hours before rolling out. Roll out the larger round of dough to an ⅛-inch thickness and place it in the pie pan; chill at least 30 minutes. Roll the other round of dough to an ⅛-inch thickness on wax paper and cut it into strips about ⅜ inch wide. Chill the strips at least 30 minutes.

Preheat the oven to 400°. Slice the peaches ½ inch thick. Toss with the blueberries. Mix the sugar, flour, and a generous grating of nutmeg. Toss with the fruit. Heap the fruit into the prepared pie pan.

Arrange a lattice over the pie with the strips of pie crust. Brush the strips with milk and sprinkle with sugar. Bake the pie with a liner pan or foil on bottom of oven to catch any juice that bubbles over. Bake about an hour until golden brown. Check the crust after 40 minutes; if it is browning too much, cover it loosely with foil. Cool the pie for at least 1 hour before serving.

SUMMER FRUIT SHORTCAKE

SERVES 8 OR 9

2 cups unbleached white flour
1 tablespoon baking powder
½ teaspoon salt
2 tablespoons sugar
8 tablespoons unsalted butter
1 cup milk
Sugar for topping
Any one of the following fruits: 1½ to 2 quarts strawberries, 1 to 1½ quarts raspberries, or 1½ pounds firm, ripe dark plums
2 to 3 teaspoons grenadine

GARNISH: 1 pint heavy cream, whipped to soft peaks, or 1 quart vanilla ice cream

Preheat the oven to 400°. Butter an 8-inch-square baking pan.

Combine the dry ingredients in a bowl or food processor. Cut 7 tablespoons of the butter into the

Luscious peach and blueberry pie is a favorite high-summer dessert.

The know-how for choosing that special peach begins at an early age in the Chesapeake area.

mixture. The butter should be the size of very small peas. Add the milk and just blend. Do not overmix.

Turn the batter into the prepared baking pan. Dot the top with the remaining tablespoon of butter. Sprinkle lightly with sugar. Bake the shortcake in the center of the oven for about 25 minutes, or until a tester comes out clean. The cake should be deep golden brown on top. Cool for 5 minutes, turn out of the pan, and split the cake horizontally.

Prepare the fruit while the cake is baking. Rinse and sort the berries or wash and stone the plums. Slice the strawberries if they are large. Slice plums about ¼ inch thick. If the fruit is tart, toss it with the grenadine, or moisten to taste.

Just before serving, cut the split cake into 8 or 9 pieces. Place a generous spoonful of fruit on each bottom piece. Add a dollop of whipped cream or a spoonful of ice cream and top with the top piece of cake. Add more fruit and whipped cream or ice cream and garnish with fruit. The cake is best if served warm, but it may be served at room temperature.

GINGER CAKES

These cakelike cookies are a third-generation family recipe given to Susan by her mother-in-law, Marguerite Ridgely Sargent.

MAKES 3 TO 4 DOZEN LARGE, SOFT GINGER COOKIES

  1 cup dark brown sugar
  5 tablespoons unsalted butter, softened
  5 tablespoons vegetable shortening
  2 extra large eggs, beaten
  ½ cup unsulfured molasses
  ½ cup prepared powdered coffee
2¾ cups unbleached white flour
  2 teaspoons baking soda
2½ teaspoons powdered ginger
  1 teaspoon cinnamon
    Generous pinch of salt

Preheat the oven to 350°. Lightly butter two baking sheets.

Cream the brown sugar with the butter and shortening. Add the eggs and blend well. Stir in the molasses, then the coffee.

Combine the dry ingredients and mix with the liquid ingredients until just blended.

Drop heaping tablespoons of dough onto the baking sheets at least 2 inches apart. The cookies spread; 12 cookies will fill a sheet. Bake for 13 to 16 minutes, until the cookies spring back when pressed lightly with a finger. Change the position of the sheets halfway through the baking.

Remove the cookies from the baking sheets and cool on racks. Store in tightly covered tins.

PEACHES AND RASPBERRIES IN CHAMPAGNE

This simple dessert requires the best quality ingredients.

SERVES 4

  3 firm, ripe, perfect peaches
  1 cup fresh raspberries
1½ cups chilled champagne, or Asti Spumante

Peel and slice the peaches. Place in a shallow dish and sprinkle with raspberries. Pour the champagne over the fruit and chill for 30 to 60 minutes. Serve the dessert chilled, but not ice cold.

BAKED APPLES WITH MAPLE SYRUP AND PECANS

SERVES 6

6 medium flavorful apples, such as Winesap or McIntosh
5 tablespoons unsalted butter
⅔ cup pure maple syrup
½ cup coarsely chopped pecans

GARNISH (optional): freshly whipped cream

Wash and core the apples, leaving the blossom end intact. Cut out a little extra flesh as you remove the cores.

Preheat the oven to 375°.

Butter a baking dish with 1 tablespoon of the butter. Melt the remaining butter with the maple syrup over low heat. Fill the apple centers loosely with the pecans. Pour the syrup and butter mixture evenly over the apples.

Bake for 30 minutes. Serve apples warm, not hot, or at room temperature, with whipped cream if you like.

PEACH ICE CREAM

MAKES ABOUT 1 QUART

1 cup half-and-half
1 cup heavy cream
⅔ to ¾ cup sugar
1 extra large egg yolk
Pinch of salt
1 pound ripe, unblemished peaches
1 teaspoon to 1 tablespoon lemon juice

Heat the half-and-half and cream with ½ cup of the sugar in a heavy saucepan over low heat until the sugar has dissolved. Beat the egg yolk lightly in a small bowl. Stir about ½ cup of the cream mixture slowly into the beaten yolk. Stir in the salt. Pour the egg mixture into the saucepan and cook the custard over low heat, stirring constantly, until it coats a metal spoon, 5 to 10 minutes.

Remove the custard from the heat and strain it into a large bowl. Set the bowl in a larger bowl containing some ice cubes. Cover the custard and set aside until it is very cold, about an hour, stirring oc-

casionally. Or place wax paper directly on the surface of the custard and cool it to room temperature. Store in the refrigerator overnight. The custard must be very cold before making the ice cream.

Peel and stone the peaches. Slice them into a bowl. Toss with the remaining sugar and lemon juice to taste. Cover the peaches and let stand about an hour.

Just before making the ice cream, puree the peaches in a food processor or blender. Adjust the flavor with sugar or lemon juice if necessary. Stir the puree into the cold custard. Pour the mixture into an ice cream maker and follow the manufacturer's directions for freezing.

PERSIMMON ICE CREAM

This is truly an out-of-the-ordinary ice cream; the flavor is delicate, yet rich.

MAKES 1½ TO 2 QUARTS

1 cup heavy cream
2 cups half-and-half
½ cup sugar
3 extra large egg yolks
Pinch of salt
2 cups persimmon puree, from approximately 5 medium to large, dead-ripe persimmons

Heat the cream, half-and-half, and sugar in a heavy-bottomed saucepan. Beat the egg yolks in a small bowl.

When the sugar has dissolved and the cream is very hot but not simmering, slowly pour about 1 cup of the cream mixture into the egg yolks and whisk well. Slowly add the yolk mixture to the cream mixture in the saucepan. Add the salt and stir well.

Cook the custard over low heat, stirring constantly, until it coats a metal spoon, 5 to 10 minutes. Strain the custard into a stainless steel bowl, place in a large bowl containing ice cubes and set aside until very cold, stirring occasionally. Or cool to lukewarm at room temperature, place wax paper directly on the custard to cover, and refrigerate. The custard should be very cold before making the ice cream.

While the custard is cooling, chill the persimmon puree. Mix the chilled custard and the puree together. Pour the mixture into an ice cream maker and follow the manufacturer's directions for freezing.

BREAD PUDDING WITH MADEIRA SAUCE

The Madeira sauce makes this rich bread pudding a little heady. We find the pudding especially toothsome when we make it with whole wheat or whole grain bread.

SERVES 6

2 cups half-and-half
1 4-inch cinnamon stick
½ teaspoon mace blades
2 tablespoons unsalted butter
2 extra large eggs, beaten lightly
⅓ cup sugar
½ teaspoon pure vanilla extract
3 cups breadcrumbs, approximately 3 slices
    bread, torn into bite-size pieces
½ cup golden raisins soaked in ½ cup Madeira
    wine
    Madeira Sauce

Preheat the oven to 350°. Butter a 1½-quart baking dish.

Scald the half-and-half with the cinnamon and mace. Stir the butter in until melted. Cool the mixture to lukewarm, then pour through a strainer. Discard the spices. Beat the eggs into the half-and-half. Stir in the sugar and the vanilla.

Put the breadcrumbs in the baking dish and pour the egg mixture over them. Drain the raisins, reserving the Madeira. Lightly toss the raisins into the bread mixture with a fork.

Place the baking dish in a larger pan and fill the pan with hot water to come halfway up the side of the dish. Bake for about 45 minutes, or until the custard is just set.

Remove from the hot water and let the pudding cool on a rack. The pudding is best served slightly warm or at room temperature, not hot or cold. Serve with the Madeira Wine Sauce or heavy cream.

MADEIRA SAUCE

MAKES A GENEROUS CUP, ENOUGH FOR
APPROXIMATELY 6 DESSERTS

6 tablespoons unsalted butter
4 tablespoons light brown sugar
1 extra large egg
½ cup Madeira

Heat the butter and sugar over moderate heat in a small, heavy-bottomed saucepan, stirring constantly.

Beat the egg in a small bowl with a whisk. Pour about half of the butter and sugar mixture into the beaten egg and whisk until well blended. Return to the saucepan and blend well.

Gradually add the Madeira, whisking well after each addition. Cook over medium-low heat, stirring frequently, until the sauce is thick and comes to a bare simmer. Do not allow the sauce to boil. Serve hot.

LEMON ANGEL CAKE WITH BLUEBERRIES AND CREAM

SERVES 8 TO 10

1 cup sifted cake flour
1¼ cups sifted sugar
1¼ cups egg whites, from 10 to 12 extra large
    eggs
1 teaspoon cream of tartar
¼ teaspoon salt
1 tablespoon lemon juice
¼ teaspoon pure vanilla extract
    Finely grated zest from 1 large lemon
1 pint blueberries, rinsed and sorted
½ pint heavy cream
    Several small sprigs lemon balm (optional)

Sift the flour three times with ½ cup of the sugar. Beat the egg whites until foamy. Sprinkle the cream of tartar and salt over the whites and beat just until soft peaks form.

Add the remaining sugar to the egg whites, 2 tablespoons at a time, beating after each addition just enough to blend. Fold in the lemon juice, vanilla, and lemon zest. Preheat the oven to 375°.

Fold the flour and sugar mixture into the beaten egg whites, about ¼ cup at a time. Fold just enough to blend.

Turn the batter gently into a 10-inch ungreased angel-food cake pan. Bake 40 to 45 minutes, until the cake is very high and golden brown on top. Invert the pan—over a bottle, if necessary—for at least 2 hours before removing the cake.

To serve, place the cake on a plate and scatter the blueberries around the cake. Whip the cream, with 2 to 3 teaspoons of sugar if desired, to very soft peaks. Serve the cream in a separate dish. If desired, garnish the platter with small lemon balm sprigs. Cut the cake with an angel-food cake knife or with 2 forks.

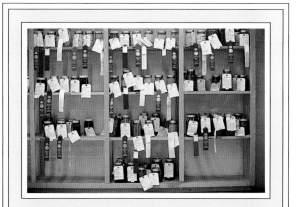

PRESERVES,
CONDIMENTS
AND
SAUCES

Just two generations ago, before the advent of freezers, the summer preserving kitchen was a feature of all but the poorest homes. It was situated to take advantage of shade trees, breezes, and the availability of water. Porches, preferably screened to keep the bees and flies at bay, were converted to summer kitchens, or outbuildings were constructed for this use. The kitchen was supplied with a wood-burning or kerosene stove, large tubs, and canning kettles. The rest of the considerable paraphernalia—canning jars, small pots, ladles, jelly bags, bowls, spoons, and tables—was moved to the site when the canning season began.

People "canned" as much as they could of fruits, vegetables, and meats. "Putting up" on a scale to feed a family of four or six during the winter was an operation that required space, careful planning, a lot of work, and close attention. Susan's neighbor, Frances Sharp, who raised five children on a dairy farm, canned every summer. She couldn't rest easy until she had at least 100 quarts of tomatoes put by. Today, Frances doesn't know how she did it: ". . . fighting the flies, which were the bane of my existence, keeping the wood stove stoked with corncobs, and feeding the family and farm help three meals a day." It helped to have willing hands—as most people did—among family and friends to share the work. Generally the men picked, harvested, and lugged the heavy boxes of produce, which the women then sorted, peeled, cut, and cooked to transform into colorful jars and bottles of preserved food.

In Frances's day, fresh produce was spiced, fermented, pickled, and juiced to assure a prodigious array of taste-tempting nourishment for winter. Jams, jellies, relishes, conserves, and pickles are still put up today, though not in the quantities of 50 years ago. Sauerkraut is no longer much preserved at home since few people remain who have knowledge of the complex curing process, and home-style sauerkraut in bulk is available at city markets. Unusual preserves such as mushroom or walnut catsup and pickled green

walnuts do not appear in many larders today, though some country people still make them from family recipes. But the preserving genius of the region still lies in converting a few basic foods into many different forms.

Tomatoes are plain-packed or made into relishes and pickles, spiced or herbed sauces, juice, or catsup. Corn is another versatile vegetable, the kernels sometimes packed plain or cream-style, but more often mixed, like cabbage, with peppers, onions, or tomatoes to make a relish. Green beans and lima beans are put up plain or with corn to make a succotash base. Both red and green peppers are favorite canning candidates, either stuffed or pickled, or as major or minor ingredients in chowchows, piccalillis, and relishes. Cucumbers are made into a variety of pickles.

Among the bounty of Chesapeake fruits, peaches are preserved in spiced sugar or brandy syrup, cooked down to make peach butter, or combined with other fruits and spices as conserves. Pitted cherries are preserved whole in the same styles as peaches, and although they are seldom mixed with other fruits, they make delicious jellies and jams on their own. Plums are also preserved whole or in conserves and chutneys. Berries—raspberries, gooseberries, blackberries, currants, and especially strawberries—thrive in this climate; even strawberry shortcake three times a week in summer leaves plenty for jams and jellies. An old method of adding pectin to the low-acid berries was to cook them with apples. This still works well, especially with raspberry and blackberry jelly; the apple flavor disappears and the jelly sets up beautifully. Apples themselves are turned into applesauce and butter, and commercially many tons are pressed into tangy, full-bodied cider.

Fruit and herb vinegars are making a reappearance after some years of lack of interest. We find them very useful for little effort.

Until this century, fruit was also commonly turned into wines or cordials. Old cookbooks offer recipes for cherry wine, blackberry wine or cordial, and gooseberry wine. One cordial we especially like is Cherry Bounce. The version we know is made by our friend Ellen Hartge, who halves the recipe in *Maryland's Way* and uses domestic sour Montmorency cherries. She recalls her aunt's Bounce, made from wild cherries, which had the tarter, more elusive flavor that uncultivated fruit always imparts.

At county fairs and in the homes of locally renowned jelly- or relish-makers, we still find evidence of the dedication and good taste that cooks such as Ellen's aunt, Nancy, and Frances Sharp brought to the necessary art of preserving.

BLACKBERRY JELLY

This jelly has an intense flavor—like blackberries picked perfectly ripe from the bush. Use a 10-quart confiture pan for this recipe. If you do not have a confiture pan, use a 6-quart noncorrodible pan and make the jelly in two batches.

MAKES 5 OR 6 HALF-PINTS

4 pints ripe blackberries
4 large tart green apples, about 2 pounds
  Sugar
  Peel from 2 lemons

Wash and pick over the blackberries. Place them in a large, noncorrodible pan and crush them a bit. Add ½ cup water. Stew over medium-low heat until the berries are quite soft, about 15 minutes.

Wash the apples, and chop coarsely, including the cores. Stew in 1 cup of water until very soft, 20 to 25 minutes.

Combine the fruits and strain through a large jelly bag or a large strainer lined with rinsed, tightly woven cheesecloth. We usually allow a large batch of fruit like this to drip overnight, so that the bag does not have to be squeezed. Stir the fruit gently with a wooden spoon to extract all of the juice. There should be about 5 cups.

Taste the juice for tartness, and add ¾ to 1 cup of sugar to every cup of juice. Add the juice and sugar mixture to the confiture pan or make the jelly in two batches. Using a vegetable peeler, remove the outer yellow peel from the lemons in strips, and add them to the pan.

Bring the mixture to a rolling boil and cook it until it sheets from a metal spoon or registers 8° above the boiling point on a thermometer. This will take about 15 minutes. Meanwhile, sterilize jelly jars, rings, and lids according to manufacturer's directions.

Skim the jelly and remove the lemon peel. Ladle the jelly into the hot, sterilized jars and seal them according to the manufacturer's directions. Cover the jars with a towel and let them come to room temperature. Check the seals, store any unsealed jars in the refrigerator, and use them as soon as possible.

GRAPE JELLY

Red, purple, or green grapes can be used to make this jelly. We often combine the red and purple grapes for a deep, rich color.

MAKES 4 OR 5 HALF-PINTS

3 pounds grapes
3 cups sugar
  Water

Wash the grapes. Leave the seeds and small stems for the pectin content. Put one layer of grapes in a large, heavy-bottomed noncorrodible pan and mash the grapes. Continue the layering and mashing with the remaining grapes. Bring to a simmer over low heat and cook for about 20 minutes.

Meanwhile, sterilize jelly jars, rings, and lids according to the manufacturer's directions.

Pour the hot mixture through a jelly bag or a large strainer lined with tightly woven cheesecloth and strain it into a bowl. Gently squeeze the cloth to obtain all of the juice.

Return the pulp to a saucepan and just cover it with water. Cook for 15 minutes and repeat the straining process, squeezing gently to extract all of the juice. There should be 4 cups of juice; if necessary, add a little water to equal this amount.

Add the juice and sugar to a clean, noncorrodible pan. Bring the mixture to a simmer; stir just until the jelly sheets from a metal spoon or reaches 8° above the boiling point of water.

Ladle the jelly into the hot, sterilized half-pint jelly jars, leaving about ⅛-inch head space. Seal the jars according to the manufacturer's directions, cover with a towel, and let cool to room temperature. Check the seals; store unsealed jars in the refrigerator and use them as soon as possible.

SOUR CHERRY JELLY

When the cherries on our tree ripen, there's a race with the birds to pick them. Almost every year we have buckets and basins of cherries to deal with all at once. Usually we make jelly to save ourselves hours of cherry-pitting. The following recipe requires a large confiture pan, and fulfills our cherry jelly obligation in one afternoon. The recipe may easily be halved for those who don't require such a high yield. If you have the cherries and the pan, make this big batch; the sweet-tart jelly disappears rapidly, and is a much appreciated gift.

MAKES APPROXIMATELY 16 HALF-PINTS

6 pounds fully ripe sour cherries
6 cups water
2 boxes fruit pectin
12 cups sugar

Sort, wash, and remove stems from cherries; do not pit them. Use a 10-quart confiture pan, or cook this recipe in two batches. Crush the cherries in the pot, add the water, and bring to a boil over high heat. Reduce the heat and simmer for 12 to 15 minutes, stirring occasionally.

Ladle the contents of the pot, in batches if necessary, into a jelly bag or a large strainer lined with tightly woven cheesecloth. We often let a large batch of fruit like this drip overnight, so that the bag does not have to be squeezed. If having really clear jelly is not important, you may gently squeeze the bag to extract all of the juice. There should be about 10 cups of liquid; add a little water, if necessary, to equal this amount.

Just before finishing the jelly, sterilize jelly jars, rings, and lids according to the manufacturer's directions.

Return the juice to the pot. Stir in the fruit pectin and bring to a full boil over high heat, stirring constantly. Immediately stir in the sugar, all at once. Stir and bring to a full rolling boil, one that cannot be stirred down. Boil for 1 minute, stirring constantly.

Remove the pan from the heat and skim the jelly if necessary. Ladle the juice into the hot, sterilized jelly jars, leaving about ⅛-inch head space. Seal the jars according to the manufacturer's directions, cover with a towel, and let cool to room temperature. Check the jars for proper seal; store unsealed jars in the refrigerator and use them as soon as possible.

RED RASPBERRY JAM

Black raspberries can be used here, though our preference is red berries because of their better flavor in jam.

MAKES 5 OR 6 HALF-PINTS

4 pints raspberries
4 cups sugar

Rinse the berries, then crush them in a heavy-bottomed, noncorrodible pot. Place over moderate heat and cook for 6 to 8 minutes, until the berries are soft. Run the berries through a food mill to remove most of the seeds. There should be about 5 cups of puree.

Meanwhile, sterilize jelly jars, rings, and lids according to the manufacturer's directions.

Return the puree to the pot, add the sugar, and stir well. Bring to a boil over moderately high heat, stirring occasionally. Cook for about 15 minutes, or just until the jam begins to sheet from a metal spoon. If a soft jam is desired, remove from the heat at this stage. If a firm jam is preferred, cook the mixture until it thickens just a bit more.

Ladle the jam into the hot, sterilized half-pint jars, leaving ¼ inch head space. Seal the jars according to the manufacturer's directions, and process the jam for 10 minutes in a boiling water bath. Remove the jars from the water, cover with a towel, and let cool to room temperature. Check the seals; store unsealed jars in the refrigerator and use them as soon as possible.

PLUM PRESERVE

This preserve can be made with any type of plum. We like to use equal quantities of red and yellow plums to create a good-flavored, ruby-red preserve.

MAKES APPROXIMATELY 4 HALF-PINTS

2 quarts ripe plums, washed, quartered, and
    pitted (about 6 cups)
3 cups sugar

Put the plums in a large, heavy-bottomed, noncorrodible pot. Place over medium heat and bring to a simmer. Stir in the sugar and cook for 20 to 30 minutes, stirring frequently. The preserve should be simmering and thickening as it cooks.

Meanwhile, sterilize canning jars, rings, and lids according to the manufacturer's directions.

When the preserve begins to sheet from a metal spoon, pour into hot, sterilized half-pint jars, leaving about ¼ inch head space. Seal the jars according to the manufacturer's directions, and process in a boiling water bath for 15 minutes. Remove the jars from the water, cover with a towel, and let cool to room temperature. Check the seals; store unsealed jars in the refrigerator and use them as soon as possible.

BLACKBERRY SYRUP

We serve this with waffles and pancakes, and over vanilla or peach ice cream. It also makes cooling summer drinks. Stir some into lemonade, or make a blackberry fizz by mixing about ¼ cup of the syrup with about 8 ounces of club soda or sparkling mineral water. The recipe may be easily doubled or tripled.

MAKES ABOUT 1 PINT

1 pint very ripe blackberries
1 cup sugar

Puree the berries and strain to remove the seeds. There should be about 2 cups of puree.

Add the puree to a noncorrodible saucepan and stir in the sugar. Bring the mixture to a simmer over medium-low heat and cook for about 15 minutes. The bubbles should barely break the surface. Pour the syrup into a sterilized pint jar or bottle. Seal the container and let it cool to room temperature. Store the syrup in the refrigerator.

You may strain the syrup after cooking it for a thinner, smoother texture. The yield will be about 1½ cups.

MRS. BESSON'S CHILI SAUCE

We think this is an excellent, versatile chili sauce. Dr. Ed Besson was reared on the Eastern Shore and belongs to a group that researches and re-creates traditional Chesapeake dishes, especially those from the region. He gave us his mother's recipe for this sauce, as well as many insights into the food and culture he knows so well.

Some tomato varieties are sweeter than others. We adjust the amount of sugar after tasting the fresh tomatoes. Many times only about half the sugar is needed.

MAKES APPROXIMATELY 5 PINTS

6 to 6½ pounds (about 18 medium) ripe tomatoes
2½ pounds (about 5 medium) onions
1½ pounds (about 3 large) sweet green peppers
½ cup sugar
2½ cups apple cider vinegar
2 teaspoons salt
1 teaspoon ground cinnamon
1 teaspoon ground allspice
1 teaspoon ground nutmeg
½ teaspoon ground cloves

Wash and core the tomatoes. Cut out soft spots if you are using canning-grade tomatoes. Peel the onions. Core and seed the peppers.

Chop the vegetables into coarse pieces and cook, covered, over medium-low heat until tender, about 40 minutes. Add the sugar, vinegar, salt, and spices; cook 10 minutes longer.

Pass the vegetables through a food mill and return to the pan. At a simmer, cook the sauce down to a fairly thick consistency. The sauce should be reduced by about one-third in 30 to 40 minutes. Stir occasionally to prevent sticking.

Meanwhile, sterilize canning jars, rings, and lids according to the manufacturer's directions.

Pour the hot sauce into the hot sterilized jars, leaving about ½ inch head space. Seal the jars, according to the manufacturer's directions, and process them in a boiling water bath for 15 minutes. Remove the jars, cover with a towel, and let cool to room temperature. Check the seals. Store unsealed jars in the refrigerator and use them as soon as possible.

FRESH TOMATO RELISH

We serve this with clams on the half shell and roasted clams, and with grilled fish.

MAKES APPROXIMATELY 2 CUPS

1 large vine-ripened tomato, about 12 ounces, diced fine
3 tablespoons grated onion
1 garlic clove, minced fine
1 tablespoon finely chopped parsley
½ teaspoon finely chopped fresh oregano
  Salt and freshly ground black pepper

Mix all the ingredients, seasoning lightly with salt and pepper. Let the relish stand at least 30 minutes before serving. It may be made a day ahead and stored, covered, in the refrigerator. Adjust the seasoning before serving at cool room temperature.

PERSIMMON AND CRANBERRY RELISH

Tart and sweet at the same time, this is a wonderful change from traditional cranberry relish.

MAKES 3½ CUPS

12 ounces (about 3 medium) dead-ripe persimmons
12 ounces cranberries
⅓ cup mild honey, or to taste
1 tablespoon Mandarine Napoleon or tangerine liqueur
  About 1½ teaspoons minced tangerine rind

Peel the persimmons and put them in a food processor. Rinse and sort the cranberries. Add to the processor with the rest of the ingredients. Pulse for about 1 minute. The relish should not be completely smooth; there should be little bits of cranberries. Refrigerate until ready to use, and serve at room temperature.

GREEN TOMATO AND CORN RELISH

MAKES APPROXIMATELY 9 PINTS

2½ pounds green tomatoes, cored and cut into ½-inch dice
2 sweet red peppers, diced
2 sweet green peppers, diced
10 to 12 ears of corn (6 or 7 cups of kernels)
3 cups diced onion
2 cups cider vinegar
5 cups water
½ cup sugar
1 tablespoon salt

BOUQUET GARNI

4 bay leaves
4 to 5 whole dried cayenne peppers
1 tablespoon coriander seed
1 tablespoon black peppercorns
2 teaspoons mustard seed

Add the vegetables to a large, noncorrodible pan with the vinegar and water. Stir in the sugar and salt. Make a bouquet garni bag of cheesecloth to hold the spices and add to the pan.

Meanwhile, sterilize canning jars, rings, and lids according to the manufacturer's directions.

Bring the relish to a simmer, stirring occasionally, for about 25 minutes. Ladle into the hot, sterilized jars, leaving ½ inch head space. Seal the jars, according to the manufacturer's directions, and process them in a boiling water bath for 5 minutes. Remove the jars, cover with a towel, and let cool to room temperature. Check the seals; store any unsealed jars in the refrigerator and use them as soon as possible. Wait at least 1 week before using the sealed jars of relish.

CRANBERRY VINEGAR

This is an unusual vinegar with a pretty color. It stands up well to reduction for sauces and is good sprinkled sparingly on sliced oranges or tangerines.

MAKES 1 PINT

12 ounces cranberries
½ cup water
¼ cup sugar
3 cups white wine or distilled vinegar

Pick over the berries and put them in a noncorrodible saucepan with the water and sugar. Cook, covered, over medium-low heat until the berries pop, about 5 minutes.

Pour the vinegar into a glass or stoneware pitcher or bowl with at least a 2-quart capacity. Add the cranberries and cover the container with a tightly woven or tripled piece of cheesecloth. Secure the cloth with a rubber band.

Keep the vinegar in a cool place away from direct sunlight for 8 days. Strain through a fine mesh strainer lined with tightly woven cheesecloth or rinsed paper toweling. Do not press the berries. Bottle the vinegar and store tightly closed. It will keep about 1 year if hermetically sealed; once opened it should be used within 6 months.

RASPBERRY VINEGAR

Homemade raspberry vinegar is much tastier than the commercial varieties, and it is easy to make. White wine vinegar gives the best result, but the raspberries greatly improve even distilled vinegar.

MAKES 1 PINT

3 cups white wine or distilled vinegar
1 pint ripe raspberries

Pour the vinegar into a glass or stoneware pitcher or bowl with at least a 2-quart capacity. Pick over the raspberries gently, rinsing if necessary. Add to the vinegar and cover the container with tightly woven or tripled cheesecloth. Secure the cloth with a rubber band.

Keep the vinegar in a cool place away from direct sunlight for 8 days. Strain through a fine mesh strainer lined with cheesecloth or rinsed paper toweling. Do not press the berries. Bottle the vinegar and store tightly closed. It will keep about 1 year if hermetically sealed; once opened it should be used within 6 months.

HONEY MUSTARD

MAKES 2 HALF-PINTS

⅓ cup mustard seed
1 cup water
½ cup Colman's mustard powder
¼ cup light honey
⅛ teaspoon salt

Soak the mustard seed in 1 cup of water for 2 hours. Drain and reserve the liquid. Grind the seed in a blender with about half of the soaking liquid for 30 seconds. Add the mustard powder, honey, salt, and the rest of the liquid. Blend to mix the mustard, about 10 seconds. The mustard will be somewhat grainy.

Pack into sterile half-pint jars and seal. Store 1 week before using. Keep refrigerated after opening.

LEMON SEAFOOD SAUCE

MAKES 1½ CUPS

1 cup Homemade Mayonnaise
2 tablespoons lemon juice, or to taste
2 tablespoons water
2 teaspoons finely chopped lemon zest
2 teaspoons Chesapeake seafood seasoning, or to taste

Mix the ingredients together, cover, and chill for at least 1 hour, or overnight. Stir before serving.

SEAFOOD HOLLANDAISE

As well as elevating simple seafood dishes, such as poached, baked, or fried white-fleshed fish, and making a rich Crab Imperial (page 120), this sauce is good with asparagus, artichokes, and poached eggs.

MAKES ¾ CUP; SERVES 4 TO 6

2 extra large eggs, beaten
5 tablespoons heavy cream
2 teaspoons lemon juice
2 teaspoons white wine vinegar
⅛ teaspoon salt
    Pinch of sugar
1 teaspoon Chesapeake seafood seasoning, or to taste
3 tablespoons unsalted butter, cut into 12 pieces

Combine all ingredients except the butter in the top of a double boiler. Place over hot, not boiling, water that does not touch the bottom of the pan. Whisk the ingredients together well. Cook, stirring constantly, until the sauce is thick, about 5 minutes.

Whisk in the butter, 2 or 3 bits at a time, until all the butter is emulsified, 2 or 3 minutes. Serve the sauce immediately, or hold it covered in the double boiler off the heat for 5 or 10 minutes.

HOMEMADE MAYONNAISE

For the finest texture, make this in a mortar or small, deep bowl, using only the egg yolk, and incorporate the oil with a pestle, whisk, or fork. The mayonnaise may also be made in a blender or food processor, using the whole egg.

MAKES APPROXIMATELY 1 CUP

1 extra large egg
1 tablespoon lemon juice
    Salt and freshly ground white pepper
¾ cup olive or vegetable oil, or a mixture

Separate out the egg yolk, or take the whole egg and beat lightly with the lemon juice and a little salt. Add the oil drop by drop, stirring constantly, until about half has been added. Add the rest of the oil in a fine stream. Adjust the seasoning with salt, freshly ground

pepper, or lemon juice to taste. Cover and refrigerate. This will keep for 3 or 4 days.

VARIATIONS: Use raspberry vinegar instead of lemon juice; add another tablespoon of vinegar to the finished mayonnaise.

Add 1 teaspoon Chesapeake seafood seasoning, or to taste, to the finished mayonnaise.

Add 1 garlic clove, minced or crushed, at the beginning of preparation.

Add 1 tablespoon finely chopped fresh herbs, especially chervil, basil, tarragon, parsley, dill weed, or coriander at the beginning of preparation for green mayonnaise, or stir into finished mayonnaise.

Add 2½ to 3 tablespoons freshly grated horseradish to finished mayonnaise.

TARTAR SAUCE

This easy-to-make sauce is lighter and tastier than commercial tartar sauces. It is good with simply prepared seafood, especially baked, grilled, or fried finfish. In the Chesapeake it also accompanies lightly seasoned crab dishes, such as Crab Cakes (page 119).

MAKES APPROXIMATELY 2½ CUPS

1 cup mayonnaise
⅔ cup sour cream
6 tablespoons finely chopped pickles (sweet, dill, cornichons, or a mixture)
3 tablespoons finely diced shallots
2 tablespoons finely chopped parsley
1 tablespoon plus 1 teaspoon capers
¼ teaspoon salt
    Freshly ground black or white pepper

Mix all ingredients together, seasoning to taste with pepper. Refrigerate and let stand at least 1 hour before serving. This sauce will keep in the refrigerator 5 or 6 days if it is tightly covered.

BIBLIOGRAPHY

Andrews, Mrs. Lewis R., and Kelly, Mrs. J. Reany, ed. *Maryland's Way*. Annapolis: The Hammond-Harwood House Association, 1963.

Bailey, Tom. *The Crab: Finding It, Catching It, and Cooking It.* Nyack, N.Y.: Rockcom Enterprises Publications, 1985.

Ball Corporation. *Ball Blue Book: The Guide to Home Canning and Freezing.* Muncie, Ind.: Ball Corporation, 1977.

Barth, John. *The Tidewater Tales.* New York: Putnam, 1987.

———. *The Sotweed Factor.* Garden City, N.Y.: Doubleday, 1967.

Beirne, Francis F. *The Amiable Baltimoreans.* Baltimore: Johns Hopkins University Press, 1951.

Bodine, A. Aubrey. *The Face of Maryland.* Baltimore: Bodine and Associates, Inc., 1961.

Bomberger, Maud. *Colonial Recipes from Old Virginia and Maryland Manors.* New York: Neale Publishing Company, 1907.

Chesapeake College Press. *The Last Hotel: Eastern Shore Summers and a Vanished Way of Life.* Wye Mills, Md.: Chesapeake College Press, 1985.

Citizens Planning and Housing Association. *Bawlamer.* Baltimore: The Livelier Baltimore Committee of the Citizens Planning and Housing Association, 1978.

Crump, Nancy. *Hearthside Cooking.* McLean, Va.: E.P.M. Publishers, 1986.

de Gast, Robert. *The Oystermen of the Chesapeake.* Camden: International Marine Publishing Company, 1970.

Department of Economic and Community Development. *Maryland Seafood Cookbooks I, II,* and *III.* Annapolis: Office of Seafood Marketing, 1976, 1982, and 1986.

Easton Maryland Memorial Hospital Junior Auxiliary. *A Cook's Tour of the Eastern Shore.* Centreville: Tidewater Publishers, 1959.

Foley, Joan, and Joe Foley. *The Chesapeake Bay Fish and Fowl Cookbook.* New York: Macmillan Publishing Company, 1981.

Geffen, Alice M., and Berglie, Carole. *Food Festival.* New York: Pantheon, 1986.

Hays, Anne M., and Hazleton, Harriet R. *Chesapeake Kaleidoscope.* Cambridge: Tidewater Publishers, 1975.

Hedeen, Robert A. *The Oyster: The Life and Lore of the Celebrated Bivalve.* Centreville: Tidewater Publishers, 1986.

Howard, Mrs. B. C. *Fifty Years in a Maryland Kitchen.* New York: Dover Publications, Inc., 1986 reprint.

Junior ·League of Baltimore. *Hunt to Harbor: An Epicurean Tour.* Baltimore: Waverly Press, Inc., 1985.

Junior League of Norfolk–Virginia Beach. *Tidewater on the Half Shell.* Atlanta: Williams Printing Company, 1985.

Kenny, Hamill. *The Origin and Meaning of the Indian Place Names of Maryland.* Baltimore: Waverly Press, Inc., 1961.

Kitching, Frances, and Dowell, Susan Stiles. *Mrs. Kitching's Smith Island Cookbook.* Centreville: Tidewater Publishers, 1981.

Latrobe, Ferdinand C. *The Chesapeake Bay Cookbook.* Baltimore: Horn-Shafer Company, 1940.

Maryland Magazine. Annapolis: Maryland Department of Economic and Employment Development.

Michener, James A. *Chesapeake.* New York: Random House, 1978.

Papenfuse, Edward C., and Stiverson, Gregory A. *Maryland: A New Guide to the Old Line State.* Baltimore: Johns Hopkins University Press, 1976.

Rollo, Vera F. *Your Maryland.* Lanham: Maryland Historical Press, 1976.

Sandler, Gilbert. *The Neighborhood: The Story of Baltimore's Little Italy.* Baltimore: Bodine and Associates, Inc., 1976.

Schaun, George, and Virginia Schaun. *Everyday Life in Colonial Maryland.* Lanham: Maryland Historical Press, 1980.

Schmidt, Whitey. *The Official Crab Eater's Guide.* Alexandria, Va.: Marian Hartness Press, 1984.

Snow, Jane Moss. *A Family Harvest, Being the Recipes and Record of Good Eating.* Indianapolis: Bobbs-Merrill, 1976.

Stieff, Frederick. *Eat, Drink, and Be Merry in Maryland.* New York: G. P. Putnam's Sons, 1932.

Tawes, Mrs. J. Millard. *My Favorite Maryland Recipes.* New York: Random House, 1964.

Tawes, William I. *God, Man, Saltwater, and the Eastern Shore.* Cambridge: Tidewater Publishers, 1977.

Warner, William W. *Beautiful Swimmers: Watermen, Crabs, and the Chesapeake Bay.* Boston: Little, Brown and Company, 1976.

Wilstach, Paul. *Tidewater Virginia.* New York: Tudor Publishing Company, 1945.

Index

frostings
  mocha buttercream, 57
  raspberry, 57
  vanilla buttercream, 49
fruit
  shortcake, summer, 162
  winter poached with persimmon
    cream, 49
  see also specific fruits

G

Gaithersburg, Md., 92
game, 12–13
  see also specific types
German-style fried noodles, 149
gingerbread, 77
gingercakes, 163
ginger nuts, 37
goose, 13
  roast Canada, 138
  salad, warm, 40
  soup, wild mushroom and, 112
goose-calling, 136, 139
goose-hunting, 13, 136
grape jelly, 169
green bean, bacon, and potato
    salad, 156
green crabs, 20
grilled
  leg of lamb with raspberry
    vinegar, 53
  marinated venison loin, 141
  soft crab with lime ginger, 121
  wild duck or dove breast with
    cranberry vinegar, 139

H

Hagerstown, Md., 92
ham, 13
  with asparagus and mustard, 88
  baked oysters and, 121
  bean soup and, 113
  and beef loaf, Besson's, 140
  biscuits with honey mustard, 68
  curing of, 4, 13, 137
  Joyce's vinegared, 73
  Southern Maryland stuffed, 45
herb farms, 2
hog-butchering, 4, 13, 152
hollandaise, seafood, 174
horseradish, 13
  beets with crème fraîche and,
    41
  bread and butter pickles with,
    76
  oysters with, 64
hot greens salad, 157
Howard County Fair, 10–11
Howard County Hunt Club, 72
hush puppies, 93

I

ice cream
  peach, 164
  persimmon, 164
International Shucking Contest,
  18

J

jellies and jams, 168–170
  blackberry, 169
  grape, 169
  plum preserve, 170
  red raspberry, 170
  sour cherry, 170

L

Ladew Topiary Gardens, 64
lamb, grilled leg of, with raspberry
    vinegar, 53
Larrilands, 144
leeks and turnips, 44
lemon seafood sauce, 173
Lexington Market (Baltimore), viii
Little Round Bay, 28
lobster
  bisque, 107
  in lettuce cups, 53
  and oyster pie, 124

M

Maryland fried chicken and cream
    gravy, 130
Maryland Hunt Cup, 52, 54
Maryland-style baked fish, 60
mayonnaise, homemade, 174
meat and game, 135–141
  see also specific types
melons, 13
  salad with crab, 154
  soup with cherries, 113